The Singer
& the Song

OTHER PUBLICATIONS
BY THE AUTHOR
Books
Preparing the Way of the Lord
God-With-Us: Resources for Prayer and Praise
Why Sing? Toward a Theology of Catholic Church Music
An Anthology of Scripture Songs
WomanPrayer, WomanSong: Resources for Ritual
WomanWord: Women of the New Testament
WomanWisdom: Women of the Hebrew Scriptures: Part One
WomanWitness: Women of the Hebrew Scriptures: Part Two
The Gospel According to Mary: A New Testament for Women
The Chronicles of Noah and Her Sisters: Genesis and Exodus According to Women
Songlines: Hymns, Songs, Rounds, and Refrains for Prayer and Praise
and
Defecting in Place: Women Claiming Responsibility
for Their Own Spiritual Lives
(co-authored with Adair Lummis and Allison Stokes)

Recordings/Published Music Collections
Joy Is Like the Rain
I Know the Secret
Knock, Knock
Seasons
Gold, Incense, and Myrrh
In Love
Mass of a Pilgrim People
RSVP: Let Us Pray
Songs of Promise
Sandstone
Remember Me
WomanSong
EarthSong
SpiritSong
Hymns Re-Imagined

Music resources are available from
Medical Mission Sisters
77 Sherman Street, Hartford, CT 06105
860-233-0875
www.medicalmissionsisters.org

MIRIAM THERESE WINTER

The Singer & the Song

An Autobiography of the Spirit

ORBIS BOOKS

Maryknoll, New York 10545

The Catholic Foreign Mission Society of America (Maryknoll) recruits and trains people for overseas missionary service. Through Orbis Books, Maryknoll aims to foster the international dialogue that is essential to mission. The books published, however, reflect the opinions of their authors and are not meant to represent the official position of the society. To obtain more information about Maryknoll or Orbis Books, please visit our website at www.maryknoll.org.

Library of Congress Cataloging-in-Publication Data
Winter, Miriam Therese.
    The singer and the song / Miriam Therese Winter.
      p. cm.
    ISBN 1-57075-279-6 (pbk.)
    1. Winter, Miriam Therese. 2. Society of Catholic Medical
Missionaries (U.S.) Biography. 3. Missionaries Biography. 4. Women
missionaries Biography. 5. Nuns – United States Biography.
    I. Title.
    BV2300.S53W55   1999
    271'.97 – dc21
    [B]   99-28617

To my mom, Irene,
from whom I received
sensitivity,
a sense of humor,
and a capacity to love,
and to my dad, Mathias,
who gave me the gift
of music
and permission
to follow my path

Contents

Preface

There comes a time in every person's life when moving forward into the future is best served by looking back. Happily ever after is integrally related to once upon a time. Steps we have taken, paths we have chosen, even paths that were chosen for us by others with or without our consent, and all those roller coaster rides of the heart are milestones on a spiritual journey that begins and ends in God. We often miss divine intent when we are caught up in the moment, while telltale signs of the Spirit, indicative of God's handiwork, emerge with remembering.

It has been a wholesome enterprise to gather up the fragments of my past. Not all of them, for who can do that, and who would even want to? Just a sampling of the more memorable moments that witness to the ubiquitous presence of the Spirit in my life. What I see as I look back are several dominant themes and a multitude of variations in a life composed in the key of change. Flowing from these are spirited improvisations inspired and encouraged by the dynamic nature of my call.

Although life is never simple, today we find ourselves in a world of increasing complexity. As one of many who will claim to have lived in two different centuries and in two distinct millennia, I seek divine intervention to keep from being pulled apart by conflicting paradigms. What was and what is about to be converge right here in the present in a crucible of contradiction. We need to take the time to embrace the pause that gives perspective, to name what we feel is essential to carry forward into the future and to begin to divest ourselves of all those life-defeating qualities that are best left behind.

An autobiography of the spirit helps us identify divine design in the twists and turns of our evolving to the place where we are now. It has done this, and more, for me. Knowing there is pattern and perhaps even purpose in what once might have seemed a mistake, or fortuitous circumstance, is a very cogent reminder that God's ways are not my ways. Grace notes from the Divine Musician have shaped the contours of my life. God's spirit leads the way and, as primary music maker, is sometimes singer, sometimes song.

You Are the Song

For as long as I can remember, I have walked and talked with God. Alone in my grandmother's garden, by the creek, in the woods, on long summer strolls down country roads far from the small, crowded tenement flat in the ethnic neighborhood of my childhood, and late into the night in the large double bed I shared with my younger sister, I would enter into the wonder-filled world of my imagination to re-create the universe, write poetry, and pray.

I was six when I first fell in love with words and the magic of metaphor. I saw that life had rhyme and rhythm and mysterious, mystical meaning. If I looked and listened hard enough, I could touch the soul of the universe and find there more than enough to satisfy my soul's insatiable craving for life beyond my own. The natural world has always been my primary sacrament, linking me to the Source of life through its intricate, intimate, infinite web of interconnectedness. Before I encountered religion, before I could say, let alone comprehend, the word "theology," before there was ever a whisper aloud about women becoming priests, I was ordained by the Spirit of God to celebrate the liturgy of life.

Although I would outwardly deny it, it was a foregone conclusion that one day I would give my life to God in some kind of radical commitment. Sure enough, shortly after high school graduation, in one swift, sweeping gesture, I left my home and family and a coveted four-year scholarship to the college of my father's dreams, left parties, pep rallies, freedom, and friends and any possibility for marriage and motherhood to enter a community unfamiliar to me to live a "religious life." I had just turned seventeen. It didn't make sense then, it doesn't now, but I knew then as I know now that it was the right choice for me.

A call to any kind of dedicated life is always an invitation. I felt that God was inviting me into an unknown future. I had only to respond. While at first that might seem daunting, in reality it simply meant saying yes to One with whom I was already in a significant relationship. "Your people will be my people." That was what I promised. "Wherever you go I will go" was God's promise to me. I gave myself completely to God and to the service of God's people, yet time would reveal that this gift of self was not quite as generous as it might at first appear.

A vocation to formal religious life was and is related to how that call is expressed. Apostolic need, community needs, an individual's strengths and inclinations are some of the factors influencing what one does or what one becomes. Religious communities have developed around a particular mission that defines and shapes their spirit and their collective contribution to the world and to the church, such as teaching, healing, care of the elderly, or the welfare and well-being of children. Individuals enter a specific community because they are drawn to its mission as seen through its good works. I wanted to be a missionary. I wanted to work in Africa. I wanted to be a doctor. Most of the communities I had heard about were primarily teaching communities, and I did not want to teach.

I am convinced it was the Spirit who led me to the Medical Mission Sisters. From the moment I saw the small brochure describing the congregation's mission, I knew this was for me. Their worldwide medical mission called for many doctors. There were missions in Africa. The entire community was dedicated to bringing professional medical care to emerging and developing nations. There was a very good chance that I too would become a doctor, and I was absolutely convinced that I would never have to teach. I had found the perfect context where I could live my life for God. I had also found a way to ensure that there was something in it for me. By choosing a community with such a focus, I had tilted the element of chance more precisely in my favor. Although I never said it quite so blatantly, I wanted to set things up so I could live for God my way.

I traveled with a friend from my home in New Jersey all the way to Philadelphia to check the community out. I did not tell my parents. The time for that would be when I was absolutely sure. As I walked down the long, tree-lined drive of the mother-house in Fox Chase in the northeast corner of Philadelphia, I knew I had come home. The fields, the farm, the forested expanse reached out to me and held me close. The community itself was energetic, innovative, and young, refreshingly unsophisticated, gracious, joyful, compassionate, and poor. I wanted to be one of them. As I watched the simple gray habits and bright blue veils weaving in and out of my line of vision, I thanked the God of my childhood faith for leading me to this place. We seemed to be a perfect match, this community and I, but had I known then in just what way, I might have remained at home.

With a trunk full of life's necessities — a dozen tins of black shoe polish, two dozen pairs of long black stockings, toothpaste, towels, and similar things — I walked away from the rest of my life on a path I had already traveled and entered a whole new world. It was a world of discovery and, much to my surprise, of liturgy and music.

I took to the sound of sacred song like a bird to the wind. As a novice, I was eager to embrace it. The modes, chants, polyphony sent my spirits soaring and gave me a taste of an everlasting splendor yet to come. The festive celebrations that marked my heart's maturing were welcome benedictions providentially bestowed. Those were the days of monastic living that we thought would never end, of first-class feasts and ferias, of manual labor and silence, of extraordinary effort to make the most of ordinary time. It wasn't always easy, and now and then it was downright hard, but for me the spiritual benefits far outweighed the deficits. As I look back I remember a time of serenity and peace.

I was well into premedical studies when the fantasy fell apart. In a series of interventions, God pruned away my preconceptions and pushed me into the real world, giving me a chance to choose again without holding back. I was told it had been decided that I would study sacred music and not anatomy. Talk of a Vatican Council and rumors of significant change had convinced my major superiors that someone would have to be prepared to help the sisters navigate the turbulent waters that lay ahead.

As a community rooted in the liturgy, we had grown up with the church's song. The rhythm of its liturgical year had shaped our identity. Medical Mission Sisters and the liturgical movement in America both began in 1925 and share a common heritage in their struggle to survive. Before receiving canonical approval as a congregation within the church, with no formal training and not a single singing voice, my community's founding pioneers huddled around a potbelly stove on many a frigid evening, rehearsing Gregorian chant. As early proponents of a marginal movement that was about to become mainstream, it would not do to suddenly say we had gone far enough.

Nevertheless, it was really quite amazing that pragmatic medical professionals who received more requests for services from those in dire medical need than our numbers could supply would decide to allow a member to focus primarily on liturgy and celebrational song. Yet they knew instinctively that someone would have to interpret, take some initiative, exercise some leadership, and teach the novices. There you have it. Teach. In Philadelphia. A silent scream, why me? I hurled it heavenward.

The choice made sense to those who were responsible for such

things. I sang in the schola, a liturgical choir. I knew how to play
the piano and for a time had accompanied our singing at Mass
on a small, single manual organ. The deciding factor, however,
was that I had a flair for liturgy and for community celebrations.
The real reason, I have come to believe, is that God had a plan
for me, and since I had not quite gotten it, the Spirit intervened.

The decision was so unusual, I was asked if I were willing, and
I could have opted out. However, saying no to my superiors at
that particular time in my life was not an option for me. So I
studied sacred music — organ, polyphony, chant — directed our
community choirs, and graduated from Catholic University with
a bachelor of music degree.

Within months after I received my degree in the traditional
Latin heritage of the universal church, the vernacular language
became mandatory for the celebration of the liturgy throughout
the United States. With the loss of Latin went the core of my
training and the clarity of my call. As for the organ, I gave my
graduation recital on a magnificent four-manual instrument with
189 stops, but once the echoes fell silent in Baltimore's Cathedral
of Mary Our Queen, I never played another note. My community
did not own an organ like professional church musicians play,
and we could never afford to buy one. We were missionaries intent on living simply in order to use all available resources for
those who are most in need.

I was assigned to teach novices at the motherhouse in Philadelphia, a task I took up with a heavy heart, extinguishing that
final flicker of hope for a mission overseas. Discouraged, disillusioned, struggling to accept the inevitable and unwilling to walk
away, I picked up a guitar that had been lying around and taught
myself some chords. It was, after all, the sixties. Folk music was
everywhere. Influenced by its accessible sound and narrative capacity, I climbed to the crest of a rolling hill where the sky
reaches to the horizon, and I began to sing.

It was a match made in heaven, the wedding of word to

a singable song, and it was life-giving for me. To sing discontent into meaning became a source of survival and therapy for the heart.

> *Come to me over the water, Peter.*
> *Walk on the waves of the storming sea.*
> *I know your boat is frail and fragile,*
> *but believe in me.*

That was the first of my folk-style songs, a refrain that led to a verse that promises:

> *I can do anything when faith doesn't weaken.*
> *See, the sea sleeps in the palm of my hand.*
> *My love's a light that leads like a beacon*
> *to the promised land.*

I sang a lot about faith and trust, and in those days, about the sea. It was an appropriate metaphor for one just barely afloat on the waves without a destination and not a star to guide me.

My tenth song marked a turning point. Grief, doubt, desperation overflowed, spilling a reservoir of pain into a simple melody that would one day echo back to me from all around the world.

> *I saw raindrops on my window,*
> *Joy is like the rain.*
> *Laughter runs across my pain,*
> *slips away and comes again.*
> *Joy is like the rain.*

My heart was literally against the wall. There was no going forward and I knew I could not go back. All these long years later, I can still hear my soul screaming: God, where are you in all of this? Why will you not help me?

> *Christ asleep within my boat,*
> *whipped by wind, yet still afloat.*
> *Joy is tried by storm.*

Suddenly, I had my answer, borne on the wind of a late spring storm as all of nature wept with me, acknowledging my defeat, holding within its fury my fear and an olive branch of hope. God is in the turbulence. God is in these changing times. God is in your helplessness. God will be with you as who God will be, as who and how you need God to be. And so I hung the rest of my life on a thread of hope and a filament of faith, and for God, that was enough.

The songs I wrote during those early days in 1965 and essentially ever after also served a ritual function. The change to vernacular language had left a hole in the liturgy that little else could fill. Without the chant's direct response to the message of the biblical word, imported hymns hung onto those texts like ill-fitting clothes out of season. I searched in vain for music that could provide an appropriate response, then began to write my own. "*I cannot come to the banquet, don't trouble me now. I have married a wife. I have bought me a cow.*" From the parable of the wedding banquet to the narrative on Zaccheus, a number of Scripture-based songs emerged to enhance our Eucharistic liturgies and, long before I realized it, were laying a path down which I would travel willingly for life.

I grew to more fully understand that all of life is sacred, that hidden deep in the world we know, the song of ages come and gone is waiting to be felt and freed. My formal training, I have come to see, was meant to help me give expression to the themes that are all around us and to proclaim these, not as peripheral, but central to the survival of the planet and me. The rhythm of the universe with its manifold improvisations, the harmonic resonance of sun and sea, the melodies of bees and birds, wind and wave, cat call and waterfall, the drumbeat of rain encountering earth, the counterpoint of the daily, of nature's sounds and human sound: this is sacred music. This is song in praise of God. Blessed are all who wholeheartedly proclaim: "I will sing to God as long as I live, sing praise to God while I have my being. God

is my strength and my song" (Ps. 104:33 and 118:14). Like the
psalter's songs, which in their day were both cultural and cultic,
so songs that arise out of life, songs that see God in secular settings, songs that people suffer to sing are truly sacred songs. I had
to experience and embrace both worlds before I could make this
claim, the world of liturgical traditions and the wider world in
which church tradition is but a miniscule part. I can name now
what I have always known, that God as primary music maker
uses various instruments to enhance the eternal song. Blessed is
the heart that yields itself to the beat of the One who drums, the
soul that vibrates to the touch of grace, the spirit open to the
breath of God making melody of us all.

I was introduced to the liturgy of the church when I entered
religious life. Its feasts were my frame of reference, and its seasons shaped my perspectives, reordering my ways. Yet I felt even
then the pull and the power of a far more primal ritual: the ring
dance of the planets, the vigil lamps of distant stars, the upraised
arms of trees in prayer, the red robe of a genuflecting sun, blood
spilling forth from the womb of day, fields ripe with food for the
spirit.

To claim one's mission and ministries is life's fundamental
challenge. Mine is a mission of healing. I sensed that as a very
young child. Although I veered away from the medical, the core
of the call is the same. I sing of One with the power to heal our
hearts and our relationships, the suffering of marginal societies,
the wounds of both past and present. Persistent healing energy is
required to erase the scars that still remain from centuries of sep-
aration within a divided church and to overcome the layer upon
layer of abuse inflicted in the name of religion. A healing presence gives grace the chance to overcome systemic injustice and
stem its destructive force, to put back together a broken world,
to comfort the suffering, encourage the dying, and root out those
self-serving attitudes that punish and plague our planet.

There are times when I am not quite certain if I am singing

the songs I sing or the songs are singing me. Perhaps it is a bit of both. I have felt the healing within whenever God is the singer and I am the song. I have also felt both joy and peace whenever I am singing and I know God is the song.

> *You spoke a word and stirred a silent spring.*
> *You touched my heart and I began to sing,*
> *to free the music deep in everything.*
> *Now all the earth with its innate melody*
> *has meaning for me forever.*
> *You are the song and You are the singing.*
> *All through the longing You come bringing music.*

◆

I saw raindrops on my window, Joy is like the rain.
Laughter runs across my pain, slips away and comes again.
Joy is like the rain.

I saw clouds upon a mountain, Joy is like a cloud.
Sometimes silver, sometimes gray, always sun not far away.
Joy is like a cloud.

I saw Christ in wind and thunder, Joy is tried by storm.
Christ asleep within my boat, whipped by wind, yet still afloat.
Joy is tried by storm.

I saw raindrops on the river, Joy is like the rain.
Bit by bit the river grows, till all at once it overflows.
Joy is like the rain.

Don't Worry

More than thirty years ago, when things in the church were about as chaotic as they appear to be now, I was all stressed out about clothes. Even as the larger theological frame was bursting at the seams of an ecclesiology that had become far too confining, even as disillusion and disaffection were raging all around, the focal point of conciliar change for me was, what would I wear? After twelve years, the biblical mandate "Don't worry about what you are to put on" had become, literally, a habit, but that was about to change.

Long before most congregations of women would address the wardrobe question, my community gave its members the option to adopt secular dress, each of us at our own pace and in a manner that best expressed our individual call to mission. It might have been easier to have been told exactly what to do, but that would not have prepared us for the world we were about to enter, one in which critical discernment and personal choice marked every step of the way.

One by one my sisters emerged, like flowers after rain — colorful, some with style, others a little frumpy — to face the modern world. I am surprised to recall, on looking back, how reluctant I was to change. It wasn't just a question of clothes; it was the issue of persona. What kind of butterfly would emerge from this veiled cocoon, I wondered. I felt like I was playing with fire, dancing dangerously close to the edge. What if my vocation went up in smoke all because of some red leather shoes? Red was my favorite color, and who knows what I might go and do when all restraints were gone?

There were also theological considerations involving the issue of sign. Who in the world would know who we were and thereby what we stood for? Now that I think back on it, who in the world really cared? Habits, we said, were a counter-cultural sign, a public expression of one's desire to disassociate from the world. That finally did it for me. The world was too much with me and I was too much into the world, in love with every aspect of the landscape of God's creation and concerned for all God's people. My place was in the midst of this world, not somewhere above or beyond it. This deeper, more self-defining habit I could not, would not change.

I chose the place of my coming out. It wouldn't be in Philadelphia, because that was where I lived. What if, among all those millions of people, I should happen to meet someone I knew while I was out buying clothes? And I wouldn't shop in a habit. Can you imagine anything more embarrassing than walking into a store with a veil and coming out with hair, and maybe even knees? Knees that were black and blue, I might add, from years of hard wooden kneelers. So I borrowed a dress and went to New York to the bargain basement at Macy's. While growing up in New Jersey, I had always heard that Macy's was the most impersonal place on earth. It was also known for its sales.

I can't remember how I looked that last day of traditional religious life, but I remember how I felt. Like a fish out of water, a soul out of synch on the sidewalks of New York. Exposed, awkward, all ankles and arms, with a tan that stopped midway at the neck and with mismatched wrists and elbows. Surely people can tell what I am, I reflected. They are thinking, "Look, there goes a nun. Doesn't she look weird?"

I was standing at a red light in downtown Manhattan, swallowed up in a sea of people, when the light changed and that immobile mob suddenly surged forward. I was caught up in its current and swept across Fifth Avenue to the opposite side of the street. In the process I experienced a series of unusual sensations. I was being shoved, literally shoved, and pushed and poked and jostled, all the way across the street. I was so surprised, I stood there, freeze-framed in a sudden burst of awareness. I had never been pushed when I wore the habit — when was the last time you shoved a nun? — nor had I felt the touch of strangers, the physical touch of a world of people for whom I had traded family life and entered into community some thirteen years before.

That moment was theologically profound. I had been given a sign about a sign on the sidewalk in front of Macy's. I had always been approachable, and my habit had not insulated me from the real world or from others, yet the world was walking around me, was treating me different from everyone else, for I myself had sent the signal that said I was set apart. I was pushed across the threshold into a deeper understanding of my dedicated life, not by those who inhabited that life, but by ordinary people who were anonymous like me.

Macy's was a madhouse. People were pushing and shoving, pushing and shoving me. After much indecision, I finally selected two dresses and a jumper and waited in line to pay, wondering who else had come to New York to purchase a change of life. The woman ahead of me, upset about something, finally walked off in a huff. Exasperated, the saleswoman turned to me and asked curtly: "Cash or charge?" Startled, I whispered, "Good afternoon. Cash. Please. Thank you." She began to ring up my purchase, when suddenly she turned, looked me straight in the eye, and asked: "What are you? Some kind of nun or something?" Horrified, I blurted out: "Why do you ask? How can you tell?" She simply said, "You're so nice."

That was all, but that was more than enough. My foolish fears of transition and change, my adolescent preoccupation with being like everyone else, my deep theological concerns about the importance of sign and symbol were all put to rest by a working woman who had been treated with respect. I left New York radically changed, not in outward appearance, but inside, where it counts. From that moment on I vowed to become the sign I had been wearing, a sign that all are called to be. It is easier to put on a habit than it is to cultivate the habit of being a loving person. The world at large will know who we are, will know we are God's disciples by our kindness and our love.

The international NGO (nongovernmental organizations) women's forum that met outside Beijing in 1995 was the result of changing habits. Women once culturally isolated and still religiously silenced proclaimed their vision of one world linked in solidarity to concerns of justice and peace. They vowed to continue networking via the Internet's World Wide Web, a giant step into the third millennium, whether we're ready for it or not. The predominant feminist initiatives came from Third World women whose perspectives reflect present trends in the universal church. It was clear to me as I followed the proceedings that the church had better change its archaic, restrictive habits or it will never understand what happened in Beijing and what is happening all around.

Patriarchy is a habit that some say cannot change, yet those of us whose patriarchal habits have undergone transformation know it can and must be done. Bishop P. Francis Murphy tried to tell this to his brother bishops in 1992:

> In our failure to come to grips with the question of patriarchy, we bishops seem to be buttoning up a coat that has the top button in the wrong button hole. No matter how carefully we button the rest of the coat, it will not fit. We cannot adjust by skipping a button. We can't pretend it fits — no matter now nice the coat.

A resounding amen from one who knows the consequences of hanging on to a habit when it no longer fits. What seemed hard to me then is ridiculous now, a necessary rite of passage into a larger reality where more critical issues were waiting and where new habits would emerge, not to inhibit, but to transform.

> *Don't worry about food or what you are to wear.*
> *Is life not more precious by far?*
> *I'll clothe you in My image and fill your emptiness*
> *and love you as you are.*
>
> *Oh, hear me! This hunger in my heart*
> *has been a craving that's consumed me from the start.*
> *Where shall I find bread that I may eat my fill*
> *and feed my weakening will?*
>
> *Oh, I drink, and still I thirst for more.*
> *I hear Your living water go rushing past my door.*
> *Give me to drink, assuage my burning thirst,*
> *and leave my soul immersed.*
>
> *I am a pauper before You now, O God.*
> *I am in tatters, my feet are unshod.*
> *I would have virtue to hide my nakedness,*
> *but who will give me dress?*

Long Road to Freedom

Ghana was my introduction to the Africa of my childhood dreams and my adolescent imagination. In the blink of an eye the pages of *National Geographic* came to life in a splash of color and confusion. Crowded markets, roadside stalls, kente and all kinds of eye-catching cloth, bananas and paw paw and parrots and yams, women with babies on their backs, at their breasts, buckets precariously perched on their heads as they walked along the long dirt roads that disappeared into the surrounding bush. It was wild and wonderful. Not even a brush with malaria could dampen my enthusiasm. I was in Africa. Once again, I had come home.

Before the end of my sojourn in Ghana, my host community decided that I should take a trip to the north. It was such a different culture, they said, with a special kind of music and liturgical adaptations that I really ought to see. Someone would accompany me. We would even go by car, starting out from our hospital in Techiman, which was already halfway there. According to miles, or kilometers, it wasn't all that far, but according to the roads in Ghana, it was a world away.

I really enjoyed the going. We stopped in Bolgatanga at its famous outdoor market where I went a little overboard buying hand-crafted things. A member of my community had said, if you ever get to Bolgatanga, pick up some things for me, and she handed me a list. Jean had a mission artifacts project back in Philadelphia. I emerged from the market laden with goods: baskets, bracelets, leather bags and beads, reed-woven musical instruments, crafts molded from metal, and carvings of ebony wood. I looked like a tinker preparing to open her very own roadside stand. It never occurred to me that I would have to haul all that baggage around. I only had to get it to Techiman, I thought, and we did have the car. Then I could ship it all home. So we stowed it and went on our way through a three-day cross-cultural whirlwind in and around Navrongo. On the third day, in the middle of the night, the real adventure began.

I was sharing a room with another sister when I awoke to see a shadow hovering over her, shaking her awake. In reality it was the shadow of death. This member of our community had traveled by public transport all the way from Techiman to bring her the tragic news that her younger brother had died in an accident in the States. It was urgent that she call her mother. The nearest transatlantic phone was in the capital city of Accra. In between Accra and Navrongo lay the entire length of Ghana. They would go together, they would leave right away, and they would take the car, but I would remain until morning. This was all conveyed in a whisper. Don't worry, I was told, I would be okay. There were very good bus connections from Bolgatanga to Techiman, with only one change, in Tamale. Our local hosts would put me on the right bus in Bolgatanga. Then I would switch to another in Tamale, one that would take me directly to our Techiman hospital gate. They said goodbye, and there I was, on my own in the north of Ghana. Three things we did not consider: that I did not know the language, that I was just about to suffer a recurrence of malaria, and that I had a lot of baggage.

When I awoke I felt really awful and was eager to make it back to more familiar surroundings, particularly if malaria a second time was to be anything like the first. The bus from Bolgatanga was to leave at six in the morning and would arrive in Tamale by eight. With luck I would be in my bed in Techiman by mid-afternoon. I was only mildly feverish and my head had not yet started to pound. It was a small discomfort compared to what my friend must be feeling at her brother's untimely death. I decided to "offer it up" and suffer in solidarity with her.

The sun had barely risen when I started out on the long road south with all of my paraphernalia, the artifacts of a proud civilization dangling from my arms, and in addition a small travel bag, my camera, and my purse. I was taken to Bolgatanga and stowed safely on the bus. It was a miserable trip. The bus was very crowded. I shivered in a draft of early morning air that blew in through a hole in the floor by my seat in the back of the bus. Every time the rickety vehicle lurched through a puddle-filled pothole I got a little wet. This too will pass, I said, and it did. I stepped out into the bright morning sun. I had made it to Tamale. Following prior instructions, I crossed the street to look for a lorry that would take me to Techiman.

The lorry park was crowded, yet before long I had located a vehicle heading for Techiman. The driver spoke a little English. I was genuinely relieved. My baggage was securely tied to the roof in typical Ghanaian fashion. I settled into a front window seat and waited to go home. And I waited. And waited. People were slowly getting on the lorry, and then they began getting off. It was well past mid-morning and I had yet to figure it out. So I called to the driver and asked, "When are we going?" "We will go," was his reply. By noon the vehicle that had been almost full was now nearly empty. "Where have the people gone?" I asked, shivering with fever. "They have gone to get something to eat," he said. And then I remembered I had brought no food, not that I was hungry. What was worse, I had brought no water, and I didn't have any money. They had bought my ticket for me in Bolgatanga and had said that the sisters would pay the driver of the second lorry on arrival in Techiman. I never thought to ask my friends where I might find something safe to drink or where I might find a latrine.

The day was slowly departing and the chance of the lorry leaving anytime soon was growing very slim. We had lost all our passengers, a point I made to the driver with a touch of hysteria. "They will come back," he assured me. "They have gone home to rest." "Will we *ever* go?" I asked, on the verge of desperation, wondering if I should make the effort to find another way home. "We will go!" he insisted. "But will we go *today?*" "Yes, we will go!" he shouted, with growing exasperation. I have long since learned that this kind of response means something different in Ghana than it does in the United States. We did not share the same assumptions. I had come from a place where we expect transportation to take us quickly from here to there. In Ghana one should not expect convenience, but rather an event. I did not know that lorries leave only when they are full, which can be today or tomorrow. The people understand this, and while they are waiting, they go about the business of life. No one was in a hurry to get anywhere in particular, no one, that is, but me.

By mid-afternoon the crowd had returned. I began to hear behind me the steady chanting of Muslim prayer, and still we did not go. By now I was really sick, and I began to cry. Quietly and unobtrusively, I thought. There was no one I could turn to. I did not know their language. I would die alone and unknown in a lorry park in Ghana. I was feeling so sorry for myself that I had not noticed that the rhythmic chanting behind me had risen to a raucous din. Suddenly the bus driver came to me and escorted me off the lorry. "Why you cry?" he demanded in an angry, accusing tone. I was so surprised, I couldn't respond. It seemed so obvious. Here I was, stuck in Tamale, when I wanted to be home in bed. "You shame me. People talk!" Indeed the prayer had turned to concern for the *bruni,* the "white one" who was crying. Somehow the people had understood the nature of my concern, and they had complained. "Why you cry?" he persisted. I could hardly tell him I was going to die, yet I did not appreciate being made to feel that the situation was my fault. "I'm sick," I said. "I need a hospital." That would surely move this vehicle on its way to Techiman. "I'll give you tablets," he responded. Then I will surely die, I thought, but said: "I don't want tablets. I want a hospital. The hospital in Techiman." "Stop crying," he said and walked away, I thought in disgust, but actually to seek some alternative transportation.

Four o'clock came and five o'clock on that awful day in Tamale. Dehydrated, shivering with chills and fever, I vaguely wondered how long I could last without a sip of water. I was slipping in and out of sleep when I saw another lorry pulling up beside our own. Men began transferring baggage. They were lifting our lorry's hood. I could not believe my eyes. There was absolutely nothing there. Now I am no mechanic, but even I could see that this lorry had no motor. Then I really began to cry. For nine long, agonizing hours, I had been sitting in a vehicle that did not have a motor. Oh, yes, we would go, but not in this lorry. Not tonight. Not all the way to Techiman. By now it was dark and once again the people began going home. How would I survive the night? "My God . . . my God . . . why have you abandoned me?" Someone was pulling my arm. The driver was pulling me off his lorry. There was all my baggage. "Hurry," he said. "Come with me." He had found a vehicle going south. He said they were willing to take me. He said it would pass through Techiman. Why should I believe anything he said? Because I was desperate.

It was a feat to move with all that baggage, but he managed to pull me, gasping, stumbling, to the rim of a small crowd. At the center of their circle stood a large modern bus. I thought it was a mirage. "Hurry, they will take you," he said, a little too nervously. "Are you sure they are going to Techiman?" I asked, not wishing to be bused to Beirut. "Yes, yes," he insisted, "see, that is for you." He was pointing to a small wooden chair being carried on to the bus. This bus has no seats, I wondered? Well, at least it had a motor. Then much to my amazement, the chair flew off the bus. It had been thrown through a window, this chair that was meant for me. The crowd became excited. People began to shout. I didn't know what they were saying. It was like a foreign film seen through a haze, a horror flick in 3D. I felt like I was going to faint with the heat and the hammering inside my head and the weight of all that baggage. "Come quick," said the voice beside me, a lot more frantically now. My ex-lorry driver was determined to put me on that bus, determined to be rid of me. Again the chair surged forward. Again it came crashing back. There was yelling all around me. My driver was pulling my arm, pulling me through the crowd to the bus, and I did not need language fluency to know that I would not be welcome there. Then suddenly, silently, from the midst of the mob and the mayhem, a small hand reached out and took my own. I looked down into the solemn eyes of a little ten-year-old girl. "You must not go," she said to me softly. "You are not wanted there." And she held on to my hand. In the strength of her gentle insistence, I cut my thin thread of hope and said: "I will not go. They do not want me on that bus." I put down my baggage, planted my feet, and watched the bus depart for Kumasi by way of Techiman, watched while my chance of survival disappeared into the encroaching night. Much later I would learn that the bus was carrying the national soccer team of Ghana to a crucial championship match. A woman on the bus? Unthinkable. Bad juju. Bad luck. I would never have been allowed on board to jinx the entire team. My driver had tried and he had failed, failed to get rid of this albatross, the source of his public shame. I would remain his responsibility until he could find transportation for me. The people on the lorry had seen to that. Not all of them had gone home.

The driver, and the little girl, finally found a vehicle going south, a small truck with open sides and canvas flaps that blew wildly in the wind and two parallel wooden slats for seats. We sat squeezed together, facing each other, like ducks lined up in a row: twenty-two Ghanaians, two large live turkeys, a mountain of baggage, and me. The truck, built to hold fourteen people, was bulging at the seams. We were packed so tight I could scarcely breathe. I was numb, but exceedingly grateful. To me this was a chariot, coming to carry me home.

Hours after the sun had set our lorry took to the pockmarked road and lumbered slowly southward. It was a long, long journey. My suffering seemed eternal. Minutes felt like years. The canvas flaps flew up and down to admit the chill night air. I had no cloth to cover my arms. I have never been so cold. My throat was parched with thirst as the fever raged within me. I thought of those trucks during World War II hauling their human cargo to the concentration camps, and I prayed to those holy people, prayed for all in prison and for all who were now in pain. Seven hours later, we arrived at the Techiman crossroads. I stood in a daze while a stranger beside me pounded on the hospital gates. One of our sisters, dressed in white, appeared like an angel of mercy. I heard her before I saw her. The last words I remember were: "We didn't think you would come this late. We've had a lot of visitors. We gave your bed away!"

I awoke in a cool, clean, borrowed bed, aware that my fever had broken, and blessed my haven of refuge and the nurturing presence of friends. I thanked God profusely, passionately — as one who was lost and has been found — for leading me safely home. As for my journey to the edge and back, the story was told, again and again, to the rippling peal of laughter. It remains a local legend, an example of how one should *never* treat a visitor from the West.

This happened years ago. In due time I recovered and the baggage was dispersed. As I continued on my journey to other parts of Africa, I reflected on that experience and saw it as an initiation rite to shake me free of assumptions that were bound to impede my understanding of peoples, cults, and cultures shaped by distinctly different worldviews. I was able to sift some significant learning from that series of events, wisdom that has contributed to my soul's constant evolving in formative or transformative ways.

The world is not enough with us. That is one of the things I learned. I had been far too circumscribed by the traditional and the familiar and by that which was said to be true, missing much of the diversity, the immensity, the serendipity of life and the unpredictable ways of God. Things change when we take the opportunity to step beyond our cultural boundaries to experience all things new. When I was on my own and no longer in control, the One-who-is took care of me in most surprising ways. So too the authentic spiritual journey is always a trip into unknown territory unrecorded on our maps. Often I find I am drawn into the depths of Mystery, into the Unknown, and I have learned that for such a journey it is best to leave all assumptions behind.

There is something else I learned. We carry too much baggage. We are caught in a mass of material things and a maze of spiritual accretion. We have so much, we need so little, yet we never seem satisfied. How many times have we had the courage to say enough is enough when faced with another's deprivation as a consequence of our greed? In the physical world and the world of the spirit we are satiated with opportunities to live in authentic relationship with God and with each other. Yet note the times we seekers of God confuse image with reality. If we are not sure Who we are looking for, how will we know when that which we are seeking has been found? The God of our tradition has been made to carry a lot of our baggage. No wonder the force of God's self-revelation is often missed or muted and the clarity of epiphany veiled.

We struggle with all our baggage, especially our interpersonal stuff. We are too caught up with pleasing others, feel guilty when we fail to perform according to their expectations or, more accurately, our own. We take too much upon ourselves, ignoring the consequences, get carried away, overextend, say yes when we should say no. As we journey through life we are overburdened with much that we do not need. For example, our assumptions and expectations are forever weighing us down. We anticipate that things will happen in the manner we expect and are confident until we encounter a situation shaped by different rules. We step into another culture, change careers or occupations, enter college or a relationship, move to another town or to another denomination, and suddenly nothing is done the way it has always been done before. It takes all our psychic energy just to hold our ground. We tend to become disoriented in situations we cannot control. Why? Because we immerse ourselves in a world of our own making. We craft our own traditions, valuing and validating only what we know. We have no basis for crossing over into cross-cultural understanding because we seldom move beyond our boundaries or step outside of ourselves. When I was stranded in Tamale, I assumed I had no one to turn to, that no one would understand, yet I was surrounded by a lorry full of sympathetic people, and in the end I was delivered by a courageous little girl.

My trip to the north taught me a lot about the essentials of the journey. It is one thing to know where we are heading, to have a sense of direction, and quite another to care about nothing else but getting there. The whole of our life is spent en route to our final destination, which means that what life is really about is what happens on the way. We may have goals, dreams, convictions, but what does all that matter if God has other plans? God or perhaps the caprice of fate may throw us a curve, force us to make a detour, to move beyond our maps. We can lose a lot of momentum when faced with the unexpected, or we can make the most of it, accepting the unanticipated as central to the ad-

venture. In Ghana I watched the marching ants intent on their
way to somewhere. Whenever they encountered an obstacle in
their path, they simply climbed over it, around it, or through it
or found another way.

If you want to be sure to get somewhere, pay attention to your
mode of travel. Vehicles are rife with assumptions. It is best to
test all assumptions, especially our religious ones. The Spirit has
taught me not to take our vehicles of grace for granted, nor to
assume that traditional sacramental channels are the only legitimate ones. Religion itself is a vehicle, one we boarded a long
time ago. We cling to certain religious practices because they
will take us where we are going, or so we have been told, yet
just because we board a vehicle bound for some destination is
no guarantee it has the necessary means to get us there. I once
held that assumption. It didn't get me very far. We can be fooled
into thinking we are moving ahead when actually we are immobile, held fast in some past paradigm or stuck in an outmoded
myth. Not every commendable conviction has the necessary mo-
tivation nor is there merit to every rite no matter how moving
the prayer. Religion can carry us forward, or it can preach a
false security that justifies standing still as we pay lip service
through lifeless forms to obsolete theologies. Feed the hungry,
free the oppressed, find housing for the homeless and opportunity
for the poor, make room for those who traditionally find themselves outside the circle, break the bread of justice, systemic and
global justice, and praise the name of the living God with a liberated heart: these are the vehicles that have the means to assure
our soul's salvation. There is always more than one way to get
where we are going, as long as we look for God in those graced
encounters along the way.

Through the process of my initiation to the world, I learned
about trust, about its link to risk and its relationship to survival.
Trust means not really knowing for sure the circumstance or its
outcome. To trust in God means to trust in God-made-manifest

through people. In Tamale where people differed from me in culture, language, and religious beliefs, I failed to trust that God often acts in ways that are unfamiliar. I did not trust nor even know my companions on the journey. I was seeking some blessed assurance along the lines of divine intervention according to predictable patterns and was rescued by a circle of strangers who in some way trusted me. The turning point came when I took the risk of trusting a little girl.

Years later I returned to Ghana and revisited Tamale. I bought some cloth from a merchant and gave it to a stranger, a woman standing by the road with a young girl beside her. She was delighted when I asked her if she would please make a dress for her daughter. And so in the spirit of gift-giving societies, the gift I had received so long ago was given back into the universe to another recipient in another form in another time in another way so the gift could keep on giving, extending the blessing beyond itself until it circles back to its source. In that place within that transcends time and all time-bound restrictions, I blessed the child who had held my hand and strengthened me in Tamale, blessed her little girl and her little girl's girls, and all of their children's children.

> *It's a long road to freedom a'winding steep and high,*
> *but when you walk in love with the wind on your wing*
> *and cover the earth with the songs you sing,*
> *the miles fly by.*
>
> *I walked one morning by the sea,*
> *and all the waves reached out to me.*
> *I took their tears, then let them be.*
>
> *I walked one morning at the dawn,*
> *when bits of night still lingered on.*
> *I sought my star, but it was gone.*

I walked one morning with a friend,
and prayed the day would never end.
The years have flown, so why pretend.

I walked one morning, marveling,
and all my winters turned to spring,
yet every moment held its sting.

Night

I have always been enthralled by nature's night music. Year after year I eagerly await the songs of insect choirs and tree frog choruses that rise up at sundown to fill the fields and woods and gardens with syncopated rhythms so insistent it seems as though the shadows themselves, and even the stars, are singing. I savor these sacred sounds of summer that transform July and August nights into musical, mystical feasts. I am also partial to the chanting of cicadas offering ambiance to the day, but there is something unique and special about the music of the night.

I was six or seven when I first claimed the night music as my soul's song. It was in the Catskill Mountains on my grandparents' farm where I spent my childhood summers communing with a natural world unknown in the inner city and unavailable to most city kids. I would lie awake at night, listening, and sometimes slip out into the darkness to be closer to the choir. Years later, the sounds amplified through a network of parks encircling the place where I was residing, I sat in the fields taking energy from the music and wrote songs of my own.

At the first sign of summer each year, my bedroom windows are thrown open in eager anticipation. Once open, they remain open, through wind and rain and sudden drops in temperature, past the first frost if need be, until the last katydid is silent and all of the choir is gone. The hardest part is waiting for the concert to begin. When will they come, I have wondered, hanging out the window late at night, forgetting that I would be far less welcoming if all or any of the insect choir actually came into the house. This year, it was almost August, and the silence was profound.

"Where are they?" I asked. "What could have happened? Do you think they are gone for good?" The query was aimed at Mary Elizabeth, a community member with whom I live and who has grown to understand how important these things are to me. "You said the same thing last year," she replied, "and as I recall, the year before that." But summer was fast departing, and I was genuinely concerned. I made a speech about environmental pollution to the administrator of the seminary — it is their house I am renting — equating fertilized green lawns with the disappearance of nature's song. When a colleague swatted an insect, I protested: "You just zapped a member of my choir." They began to wonder about me. For weeks my nightly ritual consisted of listening intently at my window for the chirp of an arthropod.

Then, one evening, I heard it. A rustle of nocturnal awakening, crickets in counterpoint, vocalizations from afar. Whether due to the heat and humidity and a spate of monsoon-like rains, or the final phase of insect growth and maturation, or simply because it was time, suddenly one night, it happened. The world around me burst into song and set my spirits singing. "We praise you, God of all the earth, and all your ways we bless," I sang, a hymn creation was singing. How grateful I was and continue to be for seemingly insignificant things that fill my life with meaning. God, who cares about the sparrows, orchestrates an opera every summer and gives the best arias to bugs. God's ways are not our ways indeed. We have much to learn from God and a whole lot to learn about music.

Why is the night music so important to me? I took some time

to reflect on this during those days when I thought I had lost it. One of the reasons has to do with linkages. It has the capacity for making connections by transcending time, space, culture, even genus and species, making all one. At a Poor Clare monastery in western Uganda in the foothills of the Mountains of the Moon, I heard that sacred sound again. As the chirping of crickets mingled with the chanting of the nuns, I was simultaneously a child of seven in the moonlight in the Catskills, a young novice chanting Compline in our Philadelphia chapel, a visitor relishing the hospitality of an African wilderness.

It brings a comforting familiarity. It is a sound that says I'm home. Wherever I go, when darkness falls, I am surrounded by a multitude of friends insisting I am not alone. The night music says I am never far from the place where I started from, that I am wrapped securely in the embrace of a God who created me and all music makers, some of whom have wings. Because of the music, night and shadows are not at all threatening. I feel safe in the dark, I love the dark — dark nights, dark spaces, dark people.

"There is nothing so dark as an African night," I wrote a while ago in Ghana, nor any people more hospitable than the inhabitants of Africa living on, above, or below its equator. The night music there also happens to be louder and far more rhythmic than any other place I have visited anywhere on earth. Darkness is a mystical metaphor for me. It generates a positive attitude which carries over to dark-skinned people everywhere. We here in America might learn something about racial harmony and equal opportunity if we could only learn to appreciate night for its own gifts and value, if we would only celebrate the dark.

Cherishing an insect's melodic offering can teach us respect and appreciation for every creature's song — yours, mine, the song of other people, the song of the animals, the planet, the galaxies within our universe and beyond. Music transmits harmony, shows us how to transpose universal truths into different modes and a variety of keys, even the key of peace. It teaches us sensitivity to differences and how to enjoy diversity. Every note is important. Every timbre is accepted. All rhythms belong.

We don't know what we have until we lose it, don't appreciate the value of something or someone until after they are gone. A quality of life is disappearing. Forests, species, cultural distinctions are disappearing. "And you shall come and hear our song and learn its tune before it fades away." This refrain from Neil Diamond's *Taproot Manuscript* sings about Africa. It is also a song about us, about our world, our ways, our legacy to all of our children's children. It is the song the insects are singing. I can hear it in my heart.

Once again summer is over, but the music lingers on. Just a little longer. Until Thanksgiving, if we are lucky, if an early frost does not silence the song. And when it does, we need to remember these words from T. S. Eliot. "We are the music, while the music lasts." In us the song continues. Through us the music lives on.

Night is the promise of morning.
Night holds the key to the dawn.
Hope is a moment embedded with stars
that shine when courage is gone,
that shine when courage is gone.

Christ on the cross saw the darkness
swallow the sweep of the earth.
Christ in the tomb held an Easter in hand
to trumpet the news of rebirth,
to trumpet the news of rebirth.

Time writes its rhythm in secret,
weaving the theme as it comes.
Death like a thief enters everyone's home,
without the beating of drums,
without the beating of drums.

Night is the promise of morning.
Night holds the key to the dawn.
Hope is a moment embedded with stars
that shine when courage is gone,
that shine when courage is gone.

Come to Me

Our house was filled to overflowing with friends who had come to Hartford for an annual women's event. As we gathered in the living room for one final philosophical fling, I lifted a large floor pillow and, much to my astonishment, uncovered a pile of broken shells from what looked like sunflower seeds. There were hundreds of them, artfully arranged, like one of those unexplained UFO mounds, and, oh, so carefully concealed from unsympathetic eyes. A mouse in the house? Worse than that. It had to be a whole convention.

I was less concerned about the mouse, or mice, than the fact that their debris had eluded mop and vacuum. The cache, a tribute to mousedom, testified to everyone present that my once-over-lightly house cleaning ways were a far cry from former times when waxed floors sparkled and windows shone. Years of convent training, along with the shards of a shattered myth, lay buried beneath the discarded shells of some stolen sunflower seeds.

I suppose I should be concerned about mice in my house, but to be honest, where would one expect them to be? Certainly not outside among the dry leaves and fallen branches. It is cold out there in February, with snow and ice and a chill wind chafing skin and fur and feather. Mice are smart and determined, which is something I learned one raw winter day at the women's prison in Niantic.

On a frigid, snow-covered afternoon, a small ball of fur suddenly scurried into the chaplain's office and huddled there, shivering and exposed. The gospel choir was rehearsing in the chapel when one of the women sounded the alarm and chaos ensued. The intruder was eventually evicted, yet before long it came in from the cold and returned to where we had found it. The little field mouse, seeking refuge in the chapel, achieved safe haven again and again despite our efforts to defeat it. There is irony in the fact that the mouse wanted in, while everyone else in that place wanted out. Two worlds converged and, for one brief moment, challenged the dominant worldview.

Life is not always what we presume and seldom as we see it. Behind what is visibly apparent lies far more than meets the eye. As part of my daily ritual, I feed the birds — yes, sunflower seeds — and have done so for some time, yet only recently have I come to realize I am also feeding mice. There are worlds parallel to the worlds we know. Behind the couch, beyond our self-absorbing routines, beyond our physical universe are the complexities of cultures and the mysteries of myriad life forms in galaxies known and as yet unknown. We discover these worlds serendipitously, perhaps through a chance encounter, or some sudden stark reminder that there is more than one mode of being, that we are virtually surrounded, not only by what we see, but also by what we cannot see.

The spirit world of angels and saints, the world of all our ancestors, the world that waits to welcome us, is pushing up against us. It is breaking in upon us. Some seem to encounter angels. Others commune with the saints or significant others who have gone before us. Yet why should we find this surprising? Our spirit longs for the realm of the spirit like a deer yearns for freshwater springs. Our spirit soars at the touch of the Spirit, transporting us between two realms, between this world and the next.

For most people this world is a haven, yet for some it holds in bondage a spirit that longs to be free. However, we belong in this world now, with all of its pain and promise, and are entrusted with its well-being. Fully aware of what is visibly present, we cannot fail to see the many blatant disparities between what is and what ought to be. While such awareness is our crucifixion, there is hope for us in the promise that beyond the cross is resurrection.

"So we do not lose heart," we are reminded, "for this slight momentary affliction is preparing us for glory which is beyond all measure, because we look not at what can be seen but at what cannot be seen; for what can be seen is temporary, but what cannot be seen is eternal" (2 Cor. 4:16–18). These words echo decisively through the centuries, giving us another perspective for a new millennium. We may end up poor as church mice, but we are rich beyond all telling, for God whose eye is on the sparrow watches over all.

So let us get our house in order. Let us discard those empty shells of outmoded religious practice and cling to the core of what really matters, God-with-us and within us. Let us live as though what is to be has already come to pass, that peace to all is latent in all, that the world itself is sanctuary offering refuge to the whole of creation. The day is fast approaching when we will be called to account for that which has been entrusted to us. On that day we will be asked not only how much we enjoyed "all things bright and beautiful," but also how we related to "all creatures great and small."

> How I have longed to draw you to Myself,
> as when a hen covets her brood,
> but you went darting like chicks in a storm,
> how could you know that My wing was warm,
> how could you know My love pursued?
> > Come to Me, my little one,
> > and you will be refreshed
> > and I will give you rest.

You'll hear Me walking on the wings of the wind,
see My warm breast in the setting sun.
Night is but shadow of My wings widespread,
My pinions preparing a bridal bed,
when all your toil and tears are done.
    Come to Me, my little one,
    and you will be refreshed
    and I will give you rest.

Know that I hover at the tip of your heart,
as a mother whose waiting is done.
Should a mother forget the child of her womb,
the joy when a loved one enters the room,
I'll not forget My cherished one.
    Come to Me, my little one,
    and you will be refreshed
    and I will give you rest.

Bread and Body Broken

I am part of an emergency rescue team in the midst of some fifty thousand survivors of the Khmer Rouge genocide. It is 1979.

In a harrowing run for freedom, innocent people, the majority of them women and children, had managed to escape annihilation by fleeing to an open field in Thailand, creating one of the first and most primitive refugee camps along the Thai-Cambodian border, a place called Sa Kaeo. Here is where I would celebrate a Christmas I would never again forget. And this is what I remember.

Advent, traditionally a season of hope and joy-filled expectation, was etched with the ravages of despair and a silent desperation. I had been assigned to one of twelve hastily erected hospital wards separating the seriously sick and those severely traumatized from the rest of the sprawling camp. The ward for tuberculosis and infectious diseases, a cramped space filled to overflowing and wide open to the elements, was to be my home for the holidays. Through long, long days and even longer nights, we managed to coax the dead back to life, the silent into speech, the isolated into human interaction. Children starving for food and affection learned to laugh again. It was exhausting, yet strangely exhilarating. Everywhere, we witnessed the tenacity of life defying all efforts to destroy it. From everyone we learned about what really matters and how much of what we thought was essential we could really do without.

We were determined to have a Christmas Eve celebration and to have it in the camp. How we would do that was far less certain. Sa Kaeo was a prison camp with armed guards and severely limited access. This was due to the infiltration of Khmer Rouge soldiers and other supporters of the genocide who were also struggling for survival. Some were patients in our ward. As relief workers, we could enter the camp, but only the hospital area, and only to fulfill our assignments. Even if we would be allowed to remain or return on Christmas Eve after our long day shifts were over, who else would want to join us for a service or a liturgy? The refugees were Buddhist. Relief workers came from many nations and had diverse religious affiliations. One of the wards was run by fundamentalist Christians, another by the Israelis, another by the Japanese. We had very little in common other than an implicit understanding that we were there to do some good.

Even though we Medical Mission Sisters longed for a Eucharistic liturgy, a Midnight Mass, we decided to prepare an ecumenical service and invite any who wished to attend, for there were many Christians who would be away from home that Christmas. Then in the final week of Advent, a Franciscan monk appeared out of nowhere. He was a French missionary working in the north who felt moved to come to the border camps to offer his services. "I thought you might need a priest," he said. Even as he spoke, I could hear the angels singing. The Spirit had decided. We would have Eucharist, and in the spirit of the One whose birth we were acknowledging, all would be welcome there.

Christmas Eve day was exhausting. After we finished our lengthy twelve-hour shift, we left the camp for the tiny hut where the ten of us were staying and had our simple evening meal of rice and vegetables. It took every shred of our energy to return to the camp that evening, yet even as we approached the gate, we could sense something was different. The guards were pleased to let us in. They even seemed excited, perhaps because Christmas is a global feast that is understood and often honored by those whose traditions differ. Or maybe it was the excitement in ourselves as in the eye of the beholder, for even the children seemed to radiate a joyous, festive spirit.

We had managed to secure a storeroom for the celebration of our liturgy. It was small, with corrugated tin walls, and adjacent to the children's ward. We could hardly hear above the din, yet the sound arising from children who had so recently been deathly silent was sheer music to our ears. We covered the floor with straw mats and left our shoes at the door, as is the custom in Thailand. I must admit, there was something definitely lacking in decor. Stacked along the walls on all three sides were large toilet tissue cartons and, on top of these, bedpans — dozens and dozens of bedpans. One of the cartons was arranged to form the table for the feast. On top was placed a white cloth, a candle in a saucer, a small chipped plate with a piece of bread, and a glass with a bit of wine. This sacred space was now prepared for our liturgical celebration, and as a lover of the liturgy, I should have been horrified. My experience in liturgical design could hardly have prepared me for a situation such as this. But then they came, relief workers seeking spiritual relief, and suddenly the decor of Christmases past, even the most elegant, could not compare with the invisible yet palpable beauty of this space.

We huddled together on the floor, crammed so tight we could scarcely move, so many of us together, despite our differences. Then the priest inquired, "What shall we sing?" I intoned the traditional carol "O Come, All You Faithful," and a dozen different languages resounded through the tiny room. The celebrant preached a homily, in French. Then he asked, "Who will speak in English?" as he looked directly at me. All of a sudden I felt all eyes turned expectantly toward me. In an instant, I was filled with dismay. I am not prepared. I have nothing to say. My blue jeans are not appropriate dress for the preaching of a sermon, a ridiculous thought in the setting. The least I can do is stand, I decided. This was not an easy achievement. Slowly, I began to rise, as my brain raced to retrieve some slice of a theology of incarnation and my heart struggled to resurrect some meaningful application. As I stood there, absolutely blank, I opened my mouth and said: "If Jesus had come to earth today, instead of two thousand years ago, he would have been born in a place like this. He would have been homeless, a refugee. He would have been born in Sa Kaeo. How privileged we are to be here." All of a sudden I realized the import of those words, and I knew this was the end of my sermon, for everything essential had been said. All present were profoundly moved by the overwhelming realization that the Christ-child born in Bethlehem was truly present here, that we had been blessed to experience the real meaning of Christmas, and that never again would we celebrate a Christmas as authentic as this.

I sat down, stunned by the insight, grateful to be united to all in the room on the level of the eternal. We cried, laughed, prayed, and sang through the remainder of the liturgy, breaking bread and breaking down the barriers that divide us, forgetting for one brief moment that we spoke different languages and understood Christ differently. We danced out into the children's ward at the close of our celebration, letting our joy spill over to delight the little ones all around.

I was convinced Christmas would never be the same for me, and, you know, it never was. I still cherish this special feast, but no matter where I am or how wonderful it is, my heart will not come home. As I sift through toys for needy children in preparation for this holy day, I feel called to preach another sermon. It is this. Whoever is disadvantaged, whoever is homeless or poor or sick or sad or in search of refuge from abuse or addiction, whoever can't be home for the holidays, whoever feels totally overwhelmed or utterly alone, remember the real meaning of Christmas: Jesus came into circumstances such as yours so that he could be there for you. For the rest of us, let us do our best to fill the Christmas season with joy and compassion and love, for that is how Jesus would have it be for every single one of us.

Architect of all creation, we Your creatures sing Your praise.
From the realm of life eternal You have fashioned finite ways.
Pale reflection of Your radiance You impart to sun and star.
From the remnants of Your Being worlds emerge and so we are.

We are drops of Living Water, we are branches of the Vine.
We are bread and body broken, we are chalice for the Wine.
Christ incarnate, we perceive You in Your manifold disguise
and are strengthened in our dyings knowing we will also rise.

Like the life force of our future or the stillness in a storm,
Holy Spirit, You are essence of all moments that transform.
When we taste the milk and honey, or the myrrh that makes us
        whole,
we say yes to Your indwelling and find solace for the soul.

God of all the generations and foundations come and gone,
in Your love we're everlasting and we will continue on.
When we seek You, we will find You in those regions where You
        dwell,
touch the wingtips of Your glory, and know more than we can tell.

Angels

It happened a long time ago, yet I can still hear Sister Claveria telling our First Communion class, as we listened intently from wooden pews, to be sure to leave some space between us for our guardian angels. Angels on the right, that's what she said, as we sat there stiffly, all in a row, so I scrunched to the left, making space for a very substantial angel. Never mind that an army of those heavenly beings could perch on the head of a pin with plenty of room to spare, something she also taught us, and if so, then why would guardian angels have to come between me and my friends? Because that's the way it was with angels, and if you wanted one, you had to make room.

How I wanted an angel beside me then, and I want one with me now. Yes, I have always believed in angels, even though, for a time, I would never admit that, even to myself. I have always had an affinity for that which lies beyond my powers of knowing. I am drawn to potential, possibility, promise. Imaginary worlds, the world of the spirit are as real to me as the physical world, and more often than not are the haven to which I retreat in times of crisis. I really believe in the communion of saints and the ever present possibility of our relating spirit to spirit. How else can we know how to live our lives here on earth as it is in heaven?

That heavenly guardians and spiritual guides are present all around us is a fact I take for granted. One could hardly grow up Catholic without encountering angelic messengers in our piety and our prayer. I especially loved the angel feasts. I would pray to Michael to protect us from evil; I would thank my personal protector on the feast of Guardian Angels; and I would whisper to Gabriel, along with Mary, "be it done to me according to your word."

Today I joyfully sing of angels who sing of peace at the birth of God's Child, sing praises with cherubim and seraphim at our Eucharistic liturgy, sing of "angels watching over me" throughout the day and "all through the night." Hark, hear "the herald angels sing" and know they are "bending near the earth," not only at Christmas time, but "all night, all day," all through the year.

Biblical evidence of angels abounds. Our liturgy resounds with the rumor of angels ascending and descending between heaven and earth, guarding the gate into paradise, wrestling us into submission, saving us from disaster, breaking the seals that shatter our assumptions, bringing us a word from God. To speak of angels has been looked upon as a religious thing, until now. Suddenly an explosion of testimony in literature and in film has blurred yet again that tenuous line between sacred and secular. More and more people from all walks of life say they have been "touched by an angel." How refreshing this turn from violent fantasies to close encounters of a spiritual kind. How encouraging for those who believe in angels but have never really seen one. Perhaps, as in that field of dreams, if we invite them, they will come.

Contemporary experience is adding a dimension to our understanding of angels. Angels are one of us. Religion, however, doesn't see it that way. We were taught that angels belong to another order of being, to the principalities and powers of the heavenly realm, and that we earthly humans were created by God a little lower than the angels. We might, and must, aspire to be saints, but we could never be angels.

Popular piety has had other ideas, then as well as now. We eagerly absorbed the information our mothers and grandmothers taught us. If we were good, if we were little angels, we would earn our halo and wings. We are called to be saints, yet time and again, we are told to act like angels. "Be an angel," we say. "You're an angel." Indeed, there are angels everywhere.

I have seen many angels throughout my life, angels of flesh and blood, the kind that never make the news. Many come at Christmas time bearing gifts for disadvantaged children: a little girl with a teddy bear nearly as big as she is; a man in his nineties with handmade wooden trains and planes and puzzles; ordinary people with wonderful toys carefully and lovingly selected; business people, women and men, with gifts they have collected from co-workers and friends. I encounter angels all the time, and in some surprising places, unknowingly earning their halos, and perhaps even wings.

Recently, one of the sisters in my community died. Brought up in the old school, Marie was somewhat prim and proper, yet her smile filled the room with light, and she had always loved my songs. As I lifted my heart to her in prayer, I was suddenly given a song. It came quite quickly, unexpectedly, as if from some other realm: "Angels, silently, wisdom unfurled, watching carefully over our world." I share the whole song with you here in gratitude for grace-laden mysteries we cannot, need not, understand.

> *Angels, silently, wisdom unfurled,*
> *watching carefully over our world,*
> *helping, hovering, guarding, and guiding:*
> *thin the veil covering angels abiding.*
>
> *Angels, unawares, into their keep,*
> *take our many cares, rock them to sleep;*
> *whisper, lovingly, words beyond knowing;*
> *sing of eternity, guiding our growing.*

Angels do begin songs that we sing,
nurture hope within till it takes wing;
link our destiny to one another,
trusting we too will be angels to others.

Angels drawing near while we're asleep,
beckon, "enter here into the deep,"
transform all regrets and empty scheming.
Their sacred silhouettes dance through our dreaming.

Angels, when we wake, come, one by one,
tasks to undertake till day is done.
Feel their tender care, masked though their form be.
Angels are everywhere. Welcome them warmly.

Angels we will see robed in shalom,
come to accompany our spirit home;
come to set us free, our last endeavor,
so that we too may be angels forever.

Hail, Little Sister

She was only in her teens and a bit naive. Well, inexperienced. She grew up in a sheltered setting. A good girl. Obedient. Religious. Reserved. Then God spoke, and that was the end of it. Gone was the age of innocence. Forever.

It was her body and her choice and she stood by her decision because she knew it was what God wanted, but that didn't make it any easier. What would she tell her father? How could she face her betrothed? Mary knew she had communed directly, intimately, with the spirit of the living God and had lived to reflect upon it. The All-Holy was now her "Beloved." Deep within her the promise was stirring: "I will be with you, always!" But what would she tell her father? Would all her uncles and male cousins insist that she be stoned? Panic may have followed those mystical moments. It very often does. Trembling, the girl-woman remembered some whispered words of assurance. Her cousin Elizabeth was also with child. Imagine. Elizabeth. Matronly, elderly Elizabeth. This was some kind of God. Not the G-d the rabbis spoke of, another reason to panic. She could think of only one thing to do. Go to Elizabeth. Stay with Elizabeth. Three months would be enough time to come up with a plan.

It would have been easy to convince her mother that they should be with Elizabeth. According to tribal custom and village

life, female relatives were expected to assist at the birth of a baby.
Did Mary confide in her mother during the long, arduous journey
from Nazareth down to the wilderness of Ein Karem? Or did she
keep her secret, only to reveal it on greeting Elizabeth through
an ecstatic outpouring of praise? One thing is certain. Knowing
her child, and seeing the aging Elizabeth with child, Anna would
have understood and been exceedingly glad. The three women
would have been there for each other, trusting that Shaddai who
had spoken would stand by the commitments they had made.

By the time she returned home to Nazareth after the birth of
Elizabeth's baby, Mary did not need words to announce the fact
of her pregnancy. Anna, no doubt, dealt with her husband after
Joachim had seen his little girl. God, meanwhile, sent an angel
to Joseph to plead on Mary's behalf. Their marriage would have
silenced any crude remarks from relatives and friends and satisfied the authorities in the synagogue and in the town. The child
who would shatter all expectations and transcend the constraints
of tradition and its laws would be legitimate, at least while in
her womb.

During the quiet months of her confinement, as Mary reflected on these things in her heart, she could never have
imagined — thank God for that — how it would all turn out. She
who was just a simple village girl would be the subject of dog-
matic promulgations and theological articulations. She would be
raised beyond all human recognition, set upon a pedestal in cavernous cathedrals and in mythologies of the mind, venerated by
monks and monarchs, by dukes and dynasties, by popes, priests,
and patriarchs, even as her gender was relegated to the status
of second class. We crowned her Queen of Heaven and Earth,
made her patron of needs and of nations, intercessor of bishops
and cardinals, of emperors and kings. We, her peers, pushed her
away, pushed her far, far away from being a part of us.

Women today doing drugs on the streets or doing time in Niantic would never turn to Mary Immaculate to get them out of a

jam or to help them change their lives. What's she know about us, they would say. She wouldn't get where we're coming from. She's had it too good, too easy — one more uppity white woman who seems to have had it all. And they say she knows absolutely nothing about sin. Then why would she mess with us?

During any given Advent, if you see the rain running down your window, think of the earth-born Mary and try to imagine her tears. Listen to her tell her story. Listen to her tell how she would like to be remembered, how she would choose to be with us now in these fitful, frightful times. Many a time I would listen and this is what I would hear.

> I am not who you think I am. I am far more than they say I am, far less than tradition proclaims I am, more human than you believe I am. I too was young once, and frightened, and very much alone. A Jewish girl, a teenage girl, pregnant and without a husband, and yes, without a lover. I never really knew the name of the father of my child. My baby was born on the streets — I was homeless at the time — and my child and I became refugees in order to survive, fleeing the wrath and the violence of one who would stalk and kill us all. My restless son never did settle down. He was always one of those visionaries chasing the impossible dream, daring to be different, daring to be like God. That's why they destroyed him. I saw the darling of my womb taken out by the weapons of fear and hate, and I witnessed his execution. I know what it feels like to be torn to shreds and to bleed inside and out. You who are on the run, who feel misunderstood, who feel judged and condemned and excluded, I understand where you are coming from. Once I felt just like you. Yet God was for me, is still for me, and with me and within me. And God is there for you, with you and within you. That is the meaning of my life, to announce that God is within you.

Thank you, Mary, sister and friend, for the powerful witness of your earthly life. Thank you for all you have meant to me, for all you continue to be for me. I pray that I too might imitate your courage to be fully, faithfully human, that I might trust the Spirit of God who speaks from down deep within me, that I might say yes to the initiatives of grace, no matter what the cost.

She walked in the summer through the heat on the hill.
She hurried as one who went with a will.
She danced in the sunlight when the day was done.
Her heart knew no evening, who carried the sun.

Fresh as a flower at the first ray of dawn,
she came to her cousin whose morning was gone.
There leaped a little child in the ancient womb,
and there leaped a little hope in every ancient tomb.

Hail, little sister, who heralds the spring.
Hail, brave mother, of whom prophets sing.
Hail to the moment beneath your breast.
May all generations call you blessed.

When you walk in the summer through the heat on the hill,
when you're wound with the wind and one with Her will,
be brave with the burden you are blessed to bear,
for it's Christ that you carry everywhere, everywhere, everywhere.

Take the Time

The flickering candle chants its litany of light into the darkness of the tiny dwelling, declaring the whole of it sacred space. Arising slowly from the ground and from a deep, hard sleep, I pause before my icon to pray. The small square hole cut out of the canvas, my window to another world, holds a silhouette of the Ethiopian bush. How peaceful just before daybreak. Too dark to distinguish the impoverished hordes huddled in the hollows of the hillsides. Too early for the silence to be shattered by the howl of hunger and cacophony of despair.

Give us this day our daily bread. Deliver us from evil. How fragile the hope that holds us hostage. Another day. Another long, hot, hard, exhausting, exasperating day. Well, better one day in Your tent, O God, O suffering, saving, compassionate God, than a thousand in the security of my own home in Connecticut. It is time to celebrate the liturgy for which I was ordained. I pull on my jeans and my thick-soled shoes. God, I believe, help my unbelief. Let all that I do praise You.

It is just after dawn and already the long, brown, deathly silent line snakes all around the perimeter of our camp and loses itself in the distance. People. Lined up for food, for work, for a handout of any kind. I don't work the camp, so it's not my job to sort out, select, and send them away. Oh, some will get work and

grain for their family. Several hundred perhaps. But there must
be a thousand already waiting and hundreds more on the way. I
drink a cup of hot tea and eat something "nourishing." A famine
biscuit with a peanut butter spread. It hardly matters. It is an
effort to swallow, seeing all those hungry people. I turn to avoid
their eyes.

As I move out into and through the crowds, lines part and
children rush to join me in procession. Together we head toward the intensive feeding center about a mile away, reenacting
the rite with the precision of routine: down to the river, across
the bridge, up the long slow hill, hot now in the morning sun,
through elephant grass and the red clay schoolyard to the tiny
compound where I will spend all my energies again in rituals of
hope and healing. A woman chanting a Muslim prayer throws
herself at my feet, and another, pleading, clings to my hand.
Women hold out their babies, thin little things, men shove small
children into my path. People pull and push, they shout, they
cry. Jesus, when you entered Jerusalem, when again and again
you encountered a crowd, how did your heart survive?

I enter the sanctuary, our place of prayer, to the chant of the
populi Deo. Their lament is loud and clear. Out of the depths of
my pain arises my own *miserere nobis*. Forgive us, O God, our sins
of insensitivity and indifference. For caring too little and possess-
ing too much. For wasting our wealth on the trivial, while the
world hangs on the cross.

The night staff comes forward to make their report. Young,
inexperienced Ethiopian villagers, desperate for work, are now
our trusted aids and "nurses." It was a fairly quiet night, they say.
Several fevers. Some distress. We are low on oil. We are out of
sugar. There is no water for the powdered milk. Why can't we
use river water? When will grain arrive from Addis? People are
hungry. I know, I say. Night shift, go home and get some sleep.
Biharu, Sultan, arrange the barrels and pray for rain. Tigiste, go
borrow two tins of oil from the Swiss camp up the road. Now let's

dish up the 8 a.m. feed, then see to medications and morning rounds.

The entrance rite is over. We move on to our liturgy. It will last at least until the end of the day and perhaps on into the night.

Several hundred life stories line the thatch walls and cover the mud floors of the three tiny rooms on the compound. Each life is a proclamation of God's word, the suffering a preaching more eloquent than any I have ever heard. The broken bodies cradle a hope and a faith that never falter. I can feel the strength all around me. I distribute food and medicines, but when it comes to the intangibles, they give and I receive. This deep, unspoken dialogue gives the message of hope its meaning. All who hunger are fed. As I move slowly around the crowded little room, greeting, touching, responding to need in my awkward, limited way, I am greeted, touched, and nurtured beyond all possible anticipation. The spirit of our incarnate God made manifest in these people caresses and calms my soul.

Our intensive feeding center for emaciated children is a temporary refuge. We set it up ourselves, Mary, Carolyn, Maura, and I. My three colleagues are nurses. I do whatever needs to be done. Daily, every two hours, what serves as bread is figuratively blessed, broken, and distributed under a variety of disguises: soybean porridge or hotcake; high protein biscuits; thick, sweet powdered milk laced with oil and sugar; and once in a while, God be praised, a very, very small banana.

Seven times a day I take, break, bless, distribute, and all around give thanks as the Author of life restores to life those physically diminished. Seven times a day, a miracle, when fully present to the Presence, I can see the shape of grace. It is 10 a.m., time once again for me to fulfill my primary daily function, presiding over a liturgy of the eucharist, presiding over the distribution of desperately needed "daily bread." When you see a hungry person and feed that person, you are feeding me, said

Jesus. I look out over the beautiful brown faces of my sisters and brothers, broken bodies with unbroken spirits. This is my body, said Jesus. Amen, I say. Amen.

That was years ago, my sojourn in Ethiopia, but in the space my heart inhabits, a space/time continuum where past, present, and future merge, the past is always with me. Somewhat like liturgical time, an empowering past is present and the celebration never ends. I am still praying prayers of petition, still searching for reconciliation, still extending greetings of peace to a host of hostile forces, still saying, over and over, words of benediction. That liturgy is not over because it is the liturgy of life and there are lessons yet to learn. I am still learning how to discern the incarnate Word in what is happening all around me, still learning how to pray the perfect prayer of forgiveness, compassion, peace. I am still learning how to be a doer of the word and not a hearer only, how in fact to *be* the word so that the message lives in me.

My associates and I are very much involved in theological education, so we look for the words to make sense of the Word as a pattern for our lives. Liturgists evaluate rites and rituals in the hope of preserving a moment in time when the sacred and secular intersect, but as denominational debates continue about rules, roles, and the proper place of women in religion, women the world over, day after day, celebrate the basic rites of life: feeding, nurturing, healing. Giving birth to life and sustaining life are truly priestly functions to which women, all women, have been divinely ordained. We spend too much time on rites arising out of our own theories and experience, when catastrophic signs in the wider world tell us to turn our attention toward a more fundamental ritual, which is the liturgy of life.

The Word awaiting proclamation has yet to be fully fathomed. The Bread of Life, already broken, must be distributed to all. Already we hear, here and there, the song of the new creation. It is a song to be improvised in which everyone has a voice. One day the whole earth, our holy earth, will be caught up in a uni-

versal dance, a cosmic celebration, because no child is hungry,
no person is in want. One day all people, having learned how
to share, will be at ease with giving thanks. At the heart of this
cosmic liturgy, of every authentic liturgy, is the God who creates
and sustains all people, the God who celebrates daily the liturgy
of life.

> Take the time to sing a song,
> for all those people who don't belong:
> the women wasted by defeat,
> the men condemned to walk the street,
> the down and out we'll never meet.
>
> Take the time to say a prayer
> for all those people who face despair:
> the starving multitudes who pray
> to make it through another day,
> who watch their children slip away.
>
> Take the time to hear the plea
> of every desperate refugee:
> the millions who have had to flee
> their lands, their loves, their liberty,
> who turn in hope to you and me.
>
> Take the time to take a stand
> for peace and justice in every land.
> Where power causes deep unrest,
> come take the part of the oppressed,
> and then, says God, you will be blessed.

Starlight

I used to love the feast of the Epiphany back in the early days when I was still somewhat cloistered. As a missionary community, we made much of the day with its emphasis on a star, a journey that required leaving one's homeland for the sake of the mission, and wisdom from the East.

Because it was a first-class feast we wore our Sunday best — a blue-gray habit and royal blue veil — prepared special choral music and a more florid *Kyrie eleison, Gloria, Credo, Sanctus, Benedictus,* and *Agnus Dei* in a melismatic mode for High Mass in the chapel. There were flowers by the statues, extra candles on the altar, and me at the tiny organ console with a prelude for the day. We had fancier food with a special dessert and talking at every meal.

Aside from Mass and community prayers, two rituals marked the occasion. The first involved discovering the kidney bean that had been hidden in one of the many cakes at our main meal. We would eat until the bean was found. The lucky one was queen for the day. I can't recall exactly what the honor entailed, but just breaking the routine and actually achieving some distinction I suspect was honor enough. The second ritual had to do with a blessing of the building in which we lived. Following a European custom, we accompanied the priest from room to room as he sprinkled the space with holy water and wrote the initials of the three kings with chalk on the lintels of the doors. You can imagine our consternation when one day the news that was spreading like wildfire had circled around to us. There weren't three kings, the rumor went. There were a whole lot more. And they weren't really kings, they were more like sages. Hardly a major milestone in the advance of human knowledge, but in those days it was akin to saying a woman could be pope. For reasons that are not quite clear, the festivities lost some of their luster, and, in time, both bean and blessings quietly disappeared. And that, I would later discover, is what epiphany really means.

What wisdom had we learned from our annual encounter with the magi and their gifts? For one thing, don't get too attached to rituals of our own making, for they may veil rather than reveal what they were meant to disclose. Epiphany means revelation, making known something previously hidden. The reason we ate our way toward indigestion in search of an elusive bean was to demonstrate that fact. But once the pattern had become routine, we preferred the bean and the status it conferred to the fundamental task of searching for the truth in God's revelatory word. The point of the magi myth is to remind us that in order to achieve a breakthrough we must leave behind those things to which we have become accustomed. We must have the courage to consider new ways no matter how alien the context, no matter how absurd the quest.

Some still miss that trinity of kings; still others never dismissed them. How in the world will we tell these folk that they never really existed, those gift-bearing savants who arrive each year in time for the holiday season. There were no kings or sages, no three or four or more wise men, no travelers from the East. At least in a literal sense. The narrative is a myth, not to be taken word for word like a poem we memorized as children, not to be anticipated image for image like a favorite home video of a major

family event. Yet that does not mean abandonment. The story is
there for the telling, a moment to be returned to, an episode to
learn from, a tradition to be loved. Knowing that the story of the
magi is a myth does not diminish its validity. It should help to
pull us closer to it as we learn to merge our own stories with the
narrative's storyline.

It is important to remember that history and myth both convey truth, but with myth the facts are fiction. Over the years I
discovered that many cherished biblical narratives are not literal
accounts of events but literary or mythic devices to engage us in
the interpretation and application of God's word. That freed me
to mine for wisdom that had previously eluded me, helped me
to see how my own experience related to the message or moved
beyond the frame.

The legend of the magi is all about moving beyond the
framework of present paradigms, with cautionary words about
consequences when those in power are challenged and their fury
is aroused. Epiphany implies that treasures of inestimable value
for which our hearts have been searching are located beyond our
reach, and we will have to stretch considerably. Those who seek
to acquire them are required to step out beyond the boundaries
of traditionally accepted standards and along uncharted paths.
T. S. Eliot, another imaginative myth maker, wrote in his poem
Journey of the Magi, "A cold coming we had of it." Cold indeed.
And lonely. And devoid of affirmation. It often is for pioneers,
for those who are courageous enough to leave what is known
behind them in search of understanding. Such is the way of wisdom. One cannot carry ephemeral securities into the unknown.
Epiphany is also about God's protection when the forces of evil
threaten the integrity of life. It has something to say to situations where the vulnerable face extinction and to anyone who
is forced into exile in order to survive. The times I've been
out to the edge and back and had to find a new way home to
protect a way of seeing and of being in the world are vivid indi-

cators to me of the myth's ability to transcend time and remain
believable.

There are also invisible boundaries we must learn to move
beyond. Liturgy is one of these. Liturgical feasts and seasons,
liturgical rites and rituals draw a line between us and them,
between religion and society and, whether intentionally or not,
between in and out, sacred and secular, between liturgy and life.
Liturgy was life before it was rite codified for the ages, and to
life we must restore it, liberating essential elements so that they
might liberate us. Epiphany is elemental to our collective and
cosmic unfolding, as the feast itself reminds us. Everywhere we
turn everything we see has potential for divine encounter and
the capacity to help us grow in wisdom and in oneness through
grace. What we learn from life's epiphanies is the reciprocity of
revelation. What is revealed to us for the good of others will be
life-transforming for those who have eyes to see. What is revealed
to and through any or all in a process that cycles forward to generation after generation will eventually be evolutionary, effecting
change at the deepest level of consciousness and communion as
our species learns how to handle not only the gold and the incense, but especially the myrrh. True epiphanies spiral on and,
in some way, limn the future. Among the most valued epiphanies are revelations to us about ourselves that contribute to our
evolving toward the best, most loving, most wholesome aspects
of our humanity.

To push beyond our interpretive frame is akin to reaching for
the stars. It takes guts to follow a star, especially one that keeps
on taking us further away from home. Starlight never falters. We
need to remember that. Beyond the far horizon, the light of grace
will enlighten us, showing some sign to mark the place where incarnate Presence dwells. In star time, God's time, distance is but
a wrinkle in time, a shift to a new dimension that gives perspective to here and now. A star, a dream, a vision — we would do
well to keep our sights on something to goad and guide us, other-

wise the enveloping void of inconsequential do's and don'ts will stalk us and swallow us whole. To follow our star, to follow our bliss is to bring epiphany down to earth where revelations matter, where ordinary folk turn to horoscopes in the absence of a vision that will evoke and energize.

Cosmologists and ecologists, physicists and theologians no longer draw a sharp distinction between planet earth and the stars. We are all cosmic matter, everything of and within planet earth and all that lies beyond it. Remember, we are stardust and to stardust we shall return. This is a fact that is already common knowledge to our children. God willing, where needed, may it be an epiphany for us.

Starlight
from afar light,
yet you are light
that lightens
our sojourning,
leave-taking,
returning.
Starlight, yours and ours:
for our love-light is one with the stars.

◆

Once upon a morning star,
when all the world was young,
before we were the way we are,
when no sad song was sung,
back in the beginning the mystery of Shalom
was known and understood:
all love returning home
to the earth, and it was, oh, so good.

Back beyond the evensong,
when time and tears lie still,
when there is no more right or wrong,
and nothing left to kill,
the memory of in the beginning will recommence
to dance the dream, and then,
earth and its lost innocence
will arise and begin it all again.

Living Water

The clouds were the last to cry in Ethiopia during that devastating drought, and when they did, I was there, to sing and dance in the rain. How good it felt to be soaked through and through with both symbol and reality. Living water. Yes, it was — filling bone-dry river beds, forming a network of tributaries to resuscitate calcified clay and entice reluctant seeds and weeds to dream of another harvest.

I have always loved the water. A morning shower cascading on me. The images of water that frequent my dreams. Creeks, brooks, lakes, streams, rivers, seas, oceans — I am drawn to these as though they were the matrix from which I have come and to which I shall return. As indeed they are, for I and my species came to birth through the womb waters of our mothers, spilling forth, as all creation, from the life-giving womb of God. One of my aims as I travel the earth is to dip my fingers and toes in all the oceans and seas of our planet, and I take delight in saying there aren't many left to go. Whether summer showers or my morning shower, it is water that restores me. The South China Sea's Great Barrier Reef, the ecological rain forests, Victoria Falls in southern Africa, the small falls of Ein Gedi by the Dead Sea below Jerusalem, an oasis in the Sinai desert, monsoon rains in the Philippines, Fiji's breakers, the Ganges in India, a creek in the Catskills, Niagara Falls, the majestic Nile, the fountains of Rome: these are some of the wonderful waters that have washed over me and nourished me and live in me forever.

There is that other side to water, as experience reminds us, the devastation and deprivation that rearrange lives and landscapes. Flood or drought, we've known both, either personally or from afar, and either extreme can kill us, or just make things so difficult that we live life sparingly.

The rains fell hard during my second stint on the Thai-Cambodia border. Children were catching fish in the streets and our tiny house was flooded. Frogs drifted through the dining area. I remember standing on the wooden steps going down to what had been the kitchen and washing my hair in the water as the suds floated away.

A year later I was in Ethiopia in the midst of drought and famine. I experienced a terrible thirst the night we ran out of drinking water. A member of our team drove to our community hospital forty kilometers away in Attat to replenish our supply. I was impatient for her return. It was a hot day, a busy day, and it had been a number of hours since I had had something to drink. Time passed and it grew dark and still no sign of the truck with its precious liquid cargo. It was not safe to drive at night. We had been warned against it. So I listened intently for the sound of the truck but heard only silence. Suddenly, there she was, the one who had gone for water, standing right behind me. Without the truck. Without the water. I was lightheaded from thirst. Could this be real, I wondered? The night had been so dark, she said, and the road unreliable. Sharp curves, massive potholes. Just as she was approaching the camp, the truck veered off the road and slid down an embankment. It came to a stop at the river's edge. It didn't go in and she was okay and for that we very grateful, but we had to have some water. With flashlights and containers we headed off into the night. She was right. It was dark. We could hear the rushing river but we never saw the water. Not that night. It was just too treacherous. One false step and we could be into something that was over our heads. We returned to the camp and went to bed. If you put a small pebble under your tongue, it helps, she whispered from behind her mosquito net. I tried it and it did. A little. How ironic, I thought to myself, as I drifted off to sleep. Too much water in Aranyaprathet and not enough in Ameya. Such is the caprice of nature with the resources that sustain us and, some have been known to say, the capriciousness of God. Yes, God gives and takes away. Still, blessed be the name of God.

The desert is the place where one really appreciates water. In the Kalahari I watched a woman poke her stick in a dry river bed and dig until it yielded a tiny pool of muddy water. Several weeks later I stepped out of the desert into the mist and spray of Victoria Falls on the great Zambezi River. An avalanche of water catapulted past, while just to the south the people struggled to find enough to drink. Deprivation. Largesse. Like coming upon hidden springs that summer in the Sinai. Isaiah and I both know what it's like to be serendipitously refreshed. In Botswana, where the Kalahari sprawls, there is but one word for water and money and blessing and rain: *pula,* a linguistic reminder of the integral association of life's necessities.

Miriam, the sister of Moses, and one with whom my spirit often identifies, lived life poised between water and wilderness. She helped to deliver her brother into the nurturing hands of Pharaoh's daughter when he lay helpless in a reed basket floating on the Nile. She led her people in a victory song after safely traversing the Sea of Reeds in their exodus from Egypt. When she died, she was buried in the oasis of Kadesh near a spring of running water. The records mention many springs, yet also say that the waters dried up for those encamped in the wilderness, suggesting that quenching physical thirst may still leave us unsatisfied, for we thirst for other things.

So many biblical stories and texts lead us to and through the waters in our search for blessedness. The Genesis narrative of the flood, for example, with its two interwoven traditions, is a myth of major importance. Within it are layers of meaning that transcend the limits of time and place. Connections between that story and our own are revealed through prayerful reflection shaped by the contours of contemporary times and our own experience. Because it is possible for us to imagine that leadership for saving the natural world is a shared responsibility, so it is we can also imagine that the covenant God made with humanity, with all creation, featured women as well as men.

We can all relate to that primeval myth from our various perspectives. How many times have we seen a world washed away before our eyes. The floods of faraway places spawned by tsunamis, cyclones, and monsoons interrupt our ease with images of devastated lives. We have seen such things closer to home as rain-swollen rivers rush to reclaim their stolen patrimony and mudslides bury a whole lot more than things we can taste and touch. Cats in boats on the evening news, rains that have been relentless — we have known our own application of those "forty days and forty nights."

We too can imagine waking up one day to face the fact that our former life with its entitlements is over, that the world we had always known and needed would never be the same again. This happens when a loved one leaves or dies or a cosmic calamity threatens. There is no going back to the way we were, no time to mourn our losses. What matters most is that we survive and then begin again.

How fortunate are those who are able to prepare for cataclysmic changes. It increases the odds of making it, perhaps even with a touch of class. The story of the flood was about many things, and these points in particular. We need to build a seafaring boat to outwit the hostile forces. We are called into relationship with all living things. Yet we are left with many questions. It is devastating to be the one to decide who will live and who will die. That happens now, somewhere in the world, among the starving and the destitute. I saw it in Ethiopia. When there's not enough food to go around, a mother tends to favor the child who has the best chance of survival. That is one of the ways, the many ways, we who are living die. While building for the future, we often make life and death choices here and now in the midst of life.

When we find ourselves adrift in life or storm-tossed on turbulent waters, that is God-given time to turn to serious introspection. When there is nowhere to go to avoid facing our fears and our feelings, no escape from our persistent needs, from our failures and misgivings, we can plumb the depths to discover the nature and source of disposable cargo. We look back on our lives to discern where and why things may have gone wrong, decide how to do things differently with the gift of a second chance. We also grab hold of the still point deep within that is our anchor and give thanks for the many blessings that provide us with the stability to ride out any storm. That is what crisis can offer us, opportunity for perspective, so necessary adjustments can be made to save what is worth saving. When the waters had receded in that time before recorded time, God made a covenant with all creation and God still does. The deluge is a rite of passage, the genesis of our coming home to ourselves and to our God. The bridge over troubled waters is the rainbow in our heart.

Each of us builds our field of dreams, but inevitably a river runs through it. Sometimes that river overflows its banks to completely overwhelm us. We are certain we won't survive. We lose our job. We lose our cool. We lose a friend or a lover. We sink in a whirlpool of emotion. We wallow in our despair. When the floodwaters threaten to destroy us, to wash away all that we cherish, we need to rise above the surface. We need to remember the rainbow, to trust that life will indeed go on, that the life that will be will be worth it. We need to let go and prepare ourselves to turn and begin again. At times such as these we have to choose the things that are worth saving. As we come face to face with life — or death — we must be able to name those things that we cannot live without.

Many Catholics thought the Mass could not survive the loss of Latin or the intrusion of a guitar, that something sacred would be utterly destroyed if we touched the host with our fingers. There were those who avoided the Bread of Life from a female Eucharistic minister. Now some feel the same about other things, like fully inclusive language, women in the pulpit, women ordained to the priesthood, or perhaps married priests. In our brief lifetime the rivers of change have washed away centuries of tradition, yet we have managed to survive.

The myth of the flood is helpful because it presents a scenario that metaphorically mirrors our own experience, giving us a chance to reflect in advance on attitudes and behavior, making sure we take into consideration the cosmic dimension of things. Life will flourish only in partnership with all creation. We go into the future two by two, yin and yang together, female and male together, religion and society together, reflection and action together, young and old, rich and poor, every culture, every race together, all living things together. Where two or more are gathered, God's spirit is there in the midst of us, God's covenant is there to strengthen us, ready and willing to rescue us and help us begin again.

Living water in the desert, in the desert, hard to find.
Living water wash the desert, wash the desert of my mind.
Still the thirst and chill the fever, source of strength, unfailing
    spring.
Cool and comfort the believer in the shadow of Your wing.

Living Water, like a river, like a fountain, like the sea.
Living Water, like a river, ever rising, rise in me.
All who thirst for Living Water turn to You, Unfailing Spring.
Wash our wounds and cleanse our spirits, Source of Life for
    everything.

We Are the Word

Sunday after Sunday, lectors in churches around the world read a text from Scripture, then say to the congregation: "This is the word of God." The intent is to take "this" literally and apply it exclusively. By "this" is meant the words themselves as recorded in the Bible. This, and only this, we are taught, is the authoritative word of God.

If we stop to think about it, we are saying that God's omnipotent word is bound within a book, limited to a set of pages, contained within certain syllables, caught between two covers, something we can hold in our hands. Primary source of revelation, we say, pointing to the Bible. All we need to know, we say, about how to live, whom to love, where to find God and the rules to follow in order to be faithful to God. Stop. Let's stop. And just think about it.

Before there was a Bible, before there were books of any kind, before they invented writing, discovered something to write with and on, members of the human race stood beneath a canopy of stars and sang of sun, trees, flowers, rippling brook and warbling bird, fruits and nuts and newborn babies and everything in their universe: "This...this...this...this...all this is of God." The early Israelites did likewise, insisting: "This is the word of God."

All life comes forth from the life of God, the will of God,

the word of God, word here being a metaphor for God's ener-gizing intervention. In the beginning, we read, is the word of God, a brooding, hovering spirit, evoking response, bringing to life, imagining all creation in an organic, evolving, unfolding pro-cess seemingly without end. The Bible itself tells us to turn our attention away from the text, to return to life and seek its source in the resources of the living. That is how the earliest traditions of the Bible understood God's creativity, namely, God's creating word. The primary source of revelation then is our world and all that is in it, our universe and all that is beyond it, all aspects of human experience and the Spirit that dwells within. Before there is a book, there is God. Life begetting life. Before, behind, within us all is God's living, everlasting word.

The process of squeezing the life out of life begins when we try to contain it and subsequently control it. Some things you just can't keep in a box or capture in a book. I believe God will give me the words to say at a time when I really need them. The gospel says something to this effect, that the Spirit will guide us in what to say in that hour when we are brought to trial for ad-hering to the spirit of Jesus. "I will give you words and a wisdom that none of your opponents will be able to withstand or con-tradict" (Luke 21:15). I could copy those words from the Bible, hang them as a poster to remind me and inspire me, but if they remain just words on a page, no matter how inspirational, no matter where they come from, they are far removed from the reality that is embedded in the text. Words come to life when someone tries to live as the words intended, not as rote repeti-tion, not to mime what has already transpired, but to reveal the truth within the words by revealing the truth within ourselves and our own experience. Scriptural words are not really words but snippets of life recorded. That means that our focus must be our lives where new words are being recorded daily in the Spirit's book of life.

We distort life when we write it down for we see only a small slice of it from a limited perspective, and who could record even that in the finite time we have? When I first went to Africa I spent six months visiting various nations throughout the continent and wrote many letters home chronicling my adventures. I also took many photos. I'll never forget my disappointment when I had the photos developed and experienced the limitations of seeing life through a lens. So much of what I had seen and experienced had fallen off at the edges as though of little consequence. As far as history is concerned those edges never existed because they are undocumented, but I know otherwise. I knew then and know better now that some of the best parts of life for me is what happens on the margins with other marginal people and events, where the cutting edge of the Spirit's thrust cuts through irrelevance and insufferable arrogance, pulling me down to where wisdom resides and the milk and honey are sweetest.

As for what I wrote, it is what I remember. What I have learned from what I wrote is that this record of my experiences and my reflection on those experiences do not have universal relevance and are, even for me, already out of date, although there may be something to learn from what I did and why. I can't help but think, however, of all that was left out, encounters in which the grace of God challenged me and changed me. What this says to me is cherish the journal because it tells me something about a past that I carry into the present, but keep it in perspective. Similarly, biblical narratives make keepsakes of experience. Like diaries, they guarantee that something will be remembered, even if we eventually forget what it was they meant to convey. We may have outgrown the particulars, in fact we most certainly have, but we treasure the memories. They have something to say to us. There are lessons to be learned from all of life, from the present and the past. The biblical past is never past; it is always a living present, not in the cultural specifics, not in the literal day-to-day data or its cumulative interpretation, but in its inner spirit, that integrating spirit in whose Spirit all are one. I rejoice that some things were written down to give us the texts of the Bible. They continue to be a measuring rod, a significant "for instance," a place to begin or return to as we evaluate our own efforts to live in the grace of God.

Some things are larger than life, and life is larger than any text that tries to tell about it. Life includes context, and context carries a subtext, which means a whole lot of living accompanies a sliver of experience. We are wise when we come to realize that our personal perspective, anyone's perspective, filters reality, rendering it already interpreted and leaving a lot unsaid. One of the precious gifts of my cross-cultural immersions has been to see life from the other side and to be nourished by new ways of comprehending and understanding. On occasion I have been blown away by some unexpected wisdom, an insight that has enabled me to see clearly for the first time what I thought I already knew. One thing I know for certain now is that God's word is a living word, a loving word, a liberating word, compassionate and inclusive. Any word that speaks otherwise is a human word, a limiting word, a vehicle of transmission and fallible interpretation.

Stowed in my storehouse of memories is a moment in time that proclaimed to me the meaning of incarnate word in all its power and its pathos. I saw clearly, instantaneously, how the biblical word is a living word because we give it flesh and meaning through the raw realities of our lives. That moment was a turning point. It left me marked for life.

Our intensive feeding center for emaciated children was in an isolated, hilly area south of Addis Ababa. We started it with a tape measure, a UNICEF scale, a large metal pot, and a ladle. We sent out word and the people came, carrying their listless little ones to the hope held out to them. Before we had a place to put them, before we even had a plan, children whose height-weight relationship was dangerously low were admitted to the circle we arranged on the ground around us. We built a fire of twigs and brush, filled the pot with water and with powdered milk we acquired somehow and would have stolen if we had to, and served drinks all around, cups of rehydrating milk to the truly destitute. We declared the center open, unwilling to wait for official word to wend its way south from Addis. In less than a week we were fully functioning and much more organized.

I saw them coming over the hill, two small specks in the distance. They arrived at the center, a woman and a man, so exhausted they barely made it, a skeleton in their arms, or so it seemed to be. Their son, they said, as they prepared to leave to go home and return with their daughter. It was hard to guess the little boy's age, he was so emaciated. "Two?" I asked. "Five," they replied. Mary took him into her arms, gave him a bit of banana and a tiny sip of milk, and declared, "He won't make it." Her years of experience in such situations led her to make that call and it would prove accurate. I, however, wanted to believe that time would show she was wrong.

The mother kept vigil beside her son, while the father went home for their little girl who was still a nursing baby. He returned late in the afternoon. I had been instructed not to give the boy too much fluid, for although he was severely dehydrated, too much too soon could kill him. However, I was also told, since he was dying anyway, I should do what I thought best to ease his suffering. The boy slipped in and out of sleep, just on the verge of coma. I sat with the family for a little while. Suddenly the boy cried, "Walga...walga." Water. Water. At that moment, time stood still. "I thirst." I heard it sound in my soul and echo through the universe. "You saw I was thirsty and gave me a drink." Biblical words, living words, Christ in the flesh of a little boy. The Christ and this child were one. A moment in time beyond time, a timeless moment trapped in time.

When I returned to the present, I did not hesitate. I gave him a sip of water. And another. And another. The mother moved away from the boy toward the child who would live, her daughter. Soon after the father also withdrew and I knew it would soon be over. They know, those who live with death, know when to let go, when to move on. I laid the boy's head in my lap and I prayed while we waited. He died later that evening. They took the body home for burial. I went with the family part of the way until the road met a path through the forest, then watched until they were gone. The mother walked on ahead alone, wailing into the night. Thank you, I whispered to the little boy as I gazed heavenward, searching for him in the stars. For the gift. For the grace of seeing and touching, and in some sense finally comprehending, the living word of God.

We call ourselves people of the book. We are not people of the book. We are people of the story. Too long have we focused on a printed page, reading the past into life, calling it forward into the present as though there were nothing now of note that might be designated gospel. Biblical stories, our stories, are one and the same story. Characters change and will continue to change in a plot that is forever evolving.

Biblical stories were once living stories similar to our stories. They lived on in oral traditions that were eventually put into writings that were collected into books that were evaluated and edited and compiled into a single volume of selected, canonical texts. The process took centuries. The texts contain not just the stories but how people felt about the stories, their own story, the collective story, and what they thought about God. Resonating throughout this process is the spirit of the living God proclaiming a liberating word within, beneath, behind human words and in the spaces in between those words where revelation hovers, waiting to reveal. The story of Jesus is part of that story. He lived, died, and lived on in spirit as the church struggled to embrace that spirit, to understand and transmit that spirit in the only way that was possible to them, through human agency. The New Testament tells their story, their understanding of the Jesus story. If we want to experience Jesus firsthand, we will have to turn to the Spirit, who is the spirit of Jesus, whose spirit lives on in us.

The Voices of Joy is a gospel choir whose song is filled with Spirit. Its members reside at the women's state prison in the sea-side town of Niantic in the state of Connecticut. They entered my life ten years ago through Selena, who founded and directs the choir, and Laurie, the prison chaplain. Selena knows about life on the streets and degrees of degradation. She spent years in and out of jail, but that was ten years ago. All that is behind her now. Gifted, funny, a woman of faith, a woman of integrity, every time she sings gospel, she is also singing the blues.

While Selena was still in prison, I invited the Voices of Joy to sing at a seminary event. The choir was allowed to go off grounds as part of a special program initiated by the prison chaplain. I watched in awe as Selena, accompanied by three other women, held a sophisticated overflow crowd spellbound in the palm of her hand. As soon as I heard the women sing, I knew I had to record them, so that they could experience the power of their own pos-sibilities. With a whole lot of help from the Spirit, I proceeded to wade through the complexities of recording a prison choir. The warden insisted I sign a paper saying I would assume all expenses. I did so, even though at the time I hadn't a cent to my name.

I decided to do half the album on location, the rest in a more controlled setting. Seven women were given clearance to join me at a local recording studio. They arrived like a flock of emanci-pated spirits, their bright, infectious energy enveloping everyone. The first of our many challenges was their uninhibited style. No holds barred, no holding back, they sang just like they lived — fast, free, and dangerously. I wish I could sing like that. They also had a tradition: everyone gets a solo song. Now that can work when you're singing live because personality can save you, but remove that personal presence and you have got to carry a tune. Six of them could, and did, and then the mike was passed to Darlene, and I cringed inwardly.

Darlene had sung just a shade off key the few times I had heard her. She was a troubled, troublesome woman, extremely uncooperative, the product of abuse and addiction. I tried to finesse her out of her role, but that was not going to happen. Sing she would and sing she did, a very long song, a tricky song, with lengthy improvisation. She sang it perfectly. I held my breath and cheered her on as she approached the ending. You came all this way, Darlene, I prayed, please don't mess up now. The final note had barely sounded when she let out a whoop of delight and relief that remains on the recording. I threw my arms around her, and she beamed as we made her the centerpiece of our recording ritual. Whoever sang a solo got to sit in the very best seat in the house, between two massive speakers at the engineer's console. This was the premier location for hearing the playback of the song, and if you were sitting in that chair, for that moment, you were the star. The expression on Darlene's face was one of sheer, unmitigated joy. "I've never done anything good," she said, repeating it over and over. Now you have, I kept telling her, and once you know you can do it, you can do good again. Between double cheeseburgers, milkshakes, and fries — gourmet food to women who had been restricted to prison fare — we laid down the tracks of all the songs that were scheduled for day one.

On the second day we took the recording studio into the prison. The choir had tripled in size. This was the best thing to happen that year, and all who qualified, even remotely, were determined not to miss it. Darlene ran to meet me, her whole personality changed. She took charge of showing me around the chapel where the choir had assembled and introduced me to Nancy, an older woman, who she said was dynamite both vocally and on the piano. We recorded the choir in between the reverberating raindrops that bounced off the pews, the railing, the floor through holes in a leaky roof. Darlene was right about Nancy. When she finished, everyone cheered. Darlene had told her all about that special ritual moment. I led her to "the soloist's seat" we had set up there on location, and as she listened to her recorded self, tears flowed, washing the wounds of self-doubt and low self-esteem. "I was in prison and you ministered to me." The words sat there incarnate. I may have visited a prison, but word made flesh and spirit reached out and ministered to me.

The money I needed walked into my office unsolicited. We threw a party at the seminary when the cassette was finally ready, and nearly all the women attended. They sang and were wildly applauded, and each received a long-stem rose from the hand of a little child. They signed autographs, just like the pros, then hurried out into the night in order to beat the curfew, headed back to the prison, Cinderellas all.

So what does this have to do with God's word? Well, frankly, everything. The down and out, the dismissed among us, are ministers now of word and song, of praise and trust and courage, a paradox, like Jesus. I had hoped the sale of the cassettes could raise a little money for the women, something to help get them started after their release, but they would have none of it. They said that all the money would go to benefit children with AIDS, and every penny has. The Voices of Joy Gospel Choir has been the largest single contributor to the Pediatrics AIDS Clinic at Yale–New Haven Hospital. Only God could have accomplished that, the spirit of God in human flesh, loving us, liberating us, speaking a word to the world through us, weaving the threads of our stories into a transforming storyline.

We are people of the story. This brings a responsibility to liberate the word of God from the linear and the literal, from the logical and cerebral, from the confines of a book. We have imprisoned the word of God, reduced the word to object status, to something we preach and teach and study and sometimes exegete, put a lid — two lids — on its power, and replaced the Spirit's two-edged sword with hieroglyphics on a page.

We must first liberate the word if we would have it liberate us. The word is not words. It is energy. It is action. It is life. It is not enough to hear God's word, not even enough to do that word, surely not enough to proclaim the word, if nothing more is to follow. You and I must *be* the word, struggle daily to become the word. We must *be* peace, compassion, love, justice, reconciliation. Don't just preach the word. Live the word. Word embodied, word enfleshed is what is meant by word incarnate. That is not a designation that is meant for Jesus only. It is not a one-time work of God but Christ's ongoing mission and God's central proclamation: that we are the word the Word proclaims, living word of our living God. Where does that leave the Scripture? Right at the heart of it all, for Scripture offers a script for life, one that requires improvisation, depends on imagination, is open to inspiration, is oriented toward transformation, not for the few or even the many. God's word is there for all.

> *Mountains and meadows and free-flowing streams,*
> *gardens and ghettoes and poor people's dreams,*
> *down through the ages the good news is heard:*
> *each of life's pages expresses the Word,*
> *love that engages enfleshes the Word.*

> *Faith moves mountains, transcending creeds.*
> *The Word within words is embodied in deeds.*
> *Fear for the future finds hope in the past,*
> *for love was the first word, it's surely the last.*

> *The poor will have privilege, the hungry will eat.*
> *All of the homeless will dance in the street.*
> *In God's revelation, real love will release*
> *the reincarnation of justice and peace.*

Food for Life

Sue, Margie, Fran, and I were sitting beside a window in a secluded alcove of a restaurant high up in the hills. This was their treat, this festive meal, to celebrate my return to the southern part of Australia. We had just completed a daylong event that had drawn a number of women. The energy and enthusiasm of our Spirit-filled rituals, the telling of our stories, the sharing of our lives lingered there among us. It was a lovely evening. The lights of the city of Adelaide shimmered and danced in the valley below. The enticing aroma of fresh baked bread, the long stem glasses of sparkling wine struck a chord deep within us. Instinctively, I took the bread, blessed it, broke it, and shared it with my sisters. As we sipped wine together, we prayed that we might remember this moment, remember the One who gave us this moment, until we could meet again.

Now the more pragmatic among us might ask, "Was that eucharist?" To which I would simply have to respond, "What is eucharist?" There is a rubric in the military that I wish were a part of the institutional church, the one where a subordinate asks, "Permission to speak freely, sir?" and is told to feel at ease. There are things about which we who are the church cannot speak freely. We are seldom at ease when we speak about things of profound significance, especially when we speak publicly about our experience of God.

Eucharist, from the Greek *eucharistia*, essentially means to give thanks. It carries a sense of celebration, of joyful, heartfelt, spontaneous praise into its applications. It is associated with Jesus, a celebration of the spirit of Jesus that was, is, and will live on with us, in us, through those of us who claim to follow him. In Christian sacramental theology, the Eucharist is core to effecting communion in the universal church and is constitutive of community. Christ is really present, and when we too are really present we become one body and are one in Spirit. The bread and cup we take and share continue a long tradition, providing an occasion to come together for good news and for nurture, to celebrate feasts and seasons, and to offer thanks and praise.

Tradition traces the Eucharist back to the last meal of Jesus with his disciples in Jerusalem just before he died, but there were also other meals that give us a glimpse of the preferences and the passionate concerns of Jesus. He preferred mixed company. He favored diversity. He broke bread, ate, and drank even with those diametrically opposed to his fundamental values. Mealtime was an inclusive time. His was a welcoming table. He sought out the unimportant ones, the crude, the crass, the criticized, those who were impoverished, those who were oppressed, those considered outcasts, and spoke out on their behalf. He confronted assumptions, broke rules, took risks, refused to conform, all in pursuit of a God-given vision of a new way of being in the world, a way that was fully inclusive, compassionate, and just. The particulars of this impossible dream were shared with those who were with him at table. Imagine the conversations. No boring chitchat there. No esoteric enclave. He chided and he challenged, called people to conversion, to reconciliation, to personal and systemic justice, all in the name of God. There must have been times when he was applauded for his unconventional teaching and disconcerting ways, times of fierce and furious debate, and times of lighthearted laughter — a dynamic table fellowship, to be sure, one that he continued up to and even beyond his death.

But was this eucharist? If these meals with Jesus were not eucharist, then I do not know what is. Bread was broken, good news shared and interpreted. Jesus the incarnate Word, Bread of Heaven, Bread of Life, was really and truly present. Bit by bit, in the heart of the individual, within an emerging community, systemically in the wider world there was substantial change. What a powerful paradigm for eucharist, a eucharist for the new millennium. It is a traditional eucharist, one with roots we can trace back to the mission and ministry of Jesus, one that can proceed parallel to and in addition to the ecclesiastical sacramental praxis of the church.

Characteristics of the common meals of Jesus during his lifetime were not those that defined the church's Eucharist after his death. Somewhere along its developmental path, Eucharist lost its domesticity, its informality, its association with an actual meal and the active participation of all present in the proclamation of the word, in the shaping of what would become our Scripture, the texts that evolved from the stories, the memories, the opinions and feelings that everybody shared. We are told that a hallmark of Eucharist in the early apostolic church was genuine *koinonia*, community in communion, where those who came together were said to be truly one, but that did not always happen. The experience of the Jerusalem church with Ananias and Sapphira, who cheated the community and then lied about it, and Paul's response to the selfish lack of sharing in the Corinthian church suggest it was otherwise (Acts 5:1–11; 1 Cor. 11:17–22). One mind, one heart, one spirit. Knowing human nature, that probably was rare. More likely, it was an ongoing struggle to be of one accord, which was a goal to strive for and not a precondition.

As sacramental practice evolved during the Middle Ages, Eucharist became a spiritual benefit for a remnant of the faithful, instead of a normative, natural way of overcoming our prejudices and learning to live with our differences, gradually, over time. The diverse and somewhat chaotic table fellowship of Jesus would seem to reflect a more realistic set of expectations for the church today, especially with regard to community, perhaps even *koinonia*. Jesus was not afraid of those who disagreed with him. In fact, the contexts in which we find him are often ones of conflict, and when it came to religion, more often than not it was Jesus who saw things differently. While Jesus remained in dialogue with his critics and even his adversaries, he himself was rebuffed or expelled simply for not conforming. The church can learn a lot from Jesus about how to deal with differences, about how to handle critics, about how to be faithful in times of change when issues related to authority and practice disrupt equilibrium. We can all learn how to take the time to work things out together, around the table, as he did.

What would the world be like, I wonder, if we recovered that ancient practice of table fellowship, if we added to our present traditions that meal tradition of Jesus, a domestic ritual parallel to our sacrament of the Eucharist but clearly distinct from it? What would our own little worlds be like if we began to celebrate eucharist as an integral part of an ordinary meal, with participants being whoever was there, whoever wished to be present, whoever needed to be present, whether or not we were of like mind or similar tradition? What forms of spirituality would emerge if our taking, breaking, and blessing bread and sharing it together set the context for conversation, for spiritual talk or spirited debate, for telling our stories, sharing concerns, discussing critical issues, for good talk, for God talk, for the gospel in our times?

Domestic eucharist with a small "e" — that is the distinction I am making here — and, yes, Christ would be present, really and truly present, for the spirit of Christ, the spirit of Jesus is present everywhere. However, and this is important to note, whether the Spirit is present to *us* would be entirely up to us.

This eucharist with a small "e" continues a Jesus tradition that differs from the Eucharist of the institutional church. In the spirit of agape, an early church practice, there would be no need for ordination. There would be no consecration. There would be open community, perhaps a rotating leadership from the youngest to the eldest, perhaps a song or a favorite hymn and a prayer of our own making. I am not describing a prayer service here, although that may be on occasion, but a brief centering ritual with a simple, integrating gesture that would set and seal the context for all subsequent interaction. The meal itself would be eucharist, begun with that opening ritual replacing our grace before our meal — short, succinct, focused — and closing with a blessing. We are so in need of a healing Spirit in our families and our communities, in our formal places of worship, in the environment where we work. Sharing a domestic eucharist can bring us closer together as a family or as friends, can help heal those wounds that inevitably lead to our wounding each other, may eventually lead the recalcitrant to a conversion of the heart. It would give us an opportunity to break open the word together and apply it to our lives. It would strengthen our resolve to live and love in the way that God intended and assuage the hunger in our hearts that only God can fill.

Eu-charis-t. At the heart of eucharist is *charis* (grace) and *charism* (gift). To do eucharist is to give thanks for the graces and gifts of the Spirit given by a gracious God. To say grace, to celebrate gifts: to give thanks for these is a grace and a gift. In the tradition of Jesus, in the Spirit of Jesus, grace before meals becomes the grace of a meal and a gift to the next generation. What a potent force for change it would be if we chose to give thanks daily in a eucharistic understanding of our common meal. A domestic eucharist movement is not so inconceivable, for our grace before meals is already in essence a eucharistic moment.

Several years ago, I was asked by a California congregation of lesbians and gays to preside and also to preach at Sunday morning worship. I made it clear that it could not be a Eucharistic service, for our denominations differed and I was not ordained. They pushed the communion table back. I took my seat in the chancel. As I waited quietly for the service to begin, I looked up at the stained-glass window. My eye caught a shaft of light falling on a Scripture verse carved into the wood of the table. The shaft of light was illuminating the words, "Do this in remembrance of me." A chill ran up my spine. What was the "this" that I would be doing in memory of Jesus? Being here, for one thing, and being fully present. I stood and asked forgiveness, in memory of Jesus, for all the anguish they had suffered in the church of Jesus Christ and especially, as a Catholic, for the wounds my tradition had inflicted on those who had once been Catholic and had since walked away. Then I spoke of peace and reconciliation in memory of him. The long, long line that stood waiting to offer me a greeting of peace at the close of the service, the tears that flowed in blessing, were eucharist for me.

Years ago in Ghana, I went to visit a traditional healer at his compound in the village. The traditional healer, or fetish priest, has often been called a witch doctor, which is inappropriate. We talked through an interpreter, even though Kofi had been to the States and was fluent in English. It was a matter of protocol. One did not address him directly when he was in a leadership role within his place of worship. I questioned him about his call and his ministry of healing, but when we began to speak about God, his interpreter fell silent. The conversation had grown too technical, too theological, for his translating skills, so Kofi poured libation, offered a prayer to Nyame, the God of gods whom we could praise together, removed his ceremonial cloth, dismissed his interpreter, and invited me outside to continue our conversation without a go-between. It was a very special exchange. He took me to his pharmacy, a thatched roof hut with a mud floor, and showed me all the healing herbs that he had artfully arranged, tiny packets, row on row, filling the wooden shelves that stood along one of the walls. "What's that?" I asked, indicating a large mound of packets strewn haphazardly on the floor. "Herbs," he replied. "Why are they on the floor?" I asked. "Because I have no more shelving."

As I prepared to depart, I thanked him for his time with me, then headed straight to the village to hire a local carpenter to make some wooden shelves. Several days later, when the shelves were completed, I asked the carpenter and his assistant if they would carry the shelving to the compound of the traditional healer. They agreed and off we went, in procession, African style, shelving up front, me behind, with children and dogs and a smattering of adults following after us, a spontaneous parade that continued to grow, typical anytime something out of the ordinary occurs. At the entrance to the compound we were joined by several of Kofi's wives and a number of his children, and then Kofi himself. "For you," I said, pointing to the shelves. "It is for your pharmacy. For the herbs that are on the floor. Now you have room for them." Then I added the following words: "I hope when you use those healing herbs, you will remember me." When my ears heard what my lips had spoken, my heart grew warm, my spirit stirred, and my soul felt satisfied.

"Do this," the rubric tells us. But what is "this" that we ought to be doing? I have asked this of the Spirit. I have asked this of myself. Feed the hungry, give drink to the thirsty, spend time with the ones who are in prison, heal the sick in body and spirit, clothe the naked, welcome the stranger into your home and into your neighborhood, liberate those who are oppressed, whose bonds have yet to be broken: do this in memory of me, do this and you will minister to me. Jesus proclaimed this again and again all around Galilee and in the streets and villages of Judea and Samaria. Do *this* unto others. This is the fast, this is the feast that Jesus asks of us.

"This is my body," Jesus said, the night of his final supper. Have you ever wondered where he was looking when he pronounced those words? At the bread he was holding in his hands? That teaching has a lengthy tradition. Well, maybe so, and maybe not. What a difference it would have made in our Eucharistic practice if we believed instead that Jesus had been looking at his disciples when he said, "This is my body." Indeed we have always known that we are the mystical body of Christ. It is we who are charged to carry out the mission and ministries of Jesus, to do good, to do justice, to live according to his spirit, to do this in memory of him. Yet we who carry out the mission are not the only ones to identify with the body of Christ. Those who are at the heart of the mission, those whom we serve and to whom we are sent are also the body of Jesus the Christ in a way we have yet to understand. For it is the teaching of Jesus that when we show compassion for others, when we promote justice for others, we do this not only in memory of Jesus but we do this for him. We do this *to* him.

My experiences in the border camps among refugees who were hungry, homeless, penniless, changed my perspective on Eucharist in ways that words can never express. A sacrament that is all about bread, about food that will satisfy hunger, can have no earthly meaning if human hungers are not addressed. The hunger for sufficient food, adequate shelter, and a modicum of respect, the hunger for love, the hunger for opportunity, for security and acceptance, for justice, peace, and reconciliation, are hungers we simply must confront in memory of Jesus. It is this we must do again and again to him, through him, for him, not only regarding those who are far from us on the other side of the planet, but those who are close, who are in our face, and are met with apathy.

"Give us this day our daily bread." Questions are sometimes raised about our eucharistic elements. Does it always have to be bread? I saw the incongruity during those times I found myself in a distinctly different culture, one in which bread was not a basic or even available. Bread in bread-eating cultures is a part of the everyday fabric of life, a fundamental staple of everybody's diet, and utterly commonplace. You can't help but see it, smell it, taste it, savor it, share it. Bread is everywhere. That's what Jesus was counting on when he gave to ordinary bread some meaningful and memorable associations to assist us in our spiritual journey. Bread would be an effective means of focusing our attention on what is really essential, that very thing in our busy lives we are most prone to forget. Our everyday bread should remind us of all we are called to be and become and all we are to accomplish. Jesus did not want us to forget that what God did through him for others, God will do through us.

So what about those places where bread is in short supply or totally unfamiliar? That is not for me to say, but if I were in Africa and part of a eucharistic meal of the type I have already described, I would look for fufu or yams, for papaya or cassava, for peanuts, maize, or mangoes, or whatever else is commonplace to the people and the place. Wherever I have been in Asia, the staple food is rice. What is important in considering the rebirth of a foundational symbol is consistency and integrity. The choice cannot be frivolous. To function in the way that bread has, the element must be one of the basic necessities of life, to be used, not once, but again and again, establishing a tradition of associations and cherished memories.

"Give us this day our daily bread." I sent the students in my graduate course on liturgy and social justice out into the city to take a homeless person to lunch the day we focused on Eucharist. I have done this several times. When members of the class included students from other faith traditions, the subject was sacramental meal. The first year, guests that were homeless got to choose the restaurant and that nearly broke the bank. In subsequent years we asked that they select within a budget because we were people with modest means, and that seemed to work out fine. Small groups of students and guests spread out to different restaurants within the city of Hartford. The meal they shared as equals was transforming and memorable, with spirited conversation, the sharing of personal stories, and a fair amount of laughter. It was a eucharist moment. The students returned with changed perspectives. "They are just like us," they told me, a point I had hoped would be apparent. An attitude based on "us" and "them" had shifted during the meal. They told about the looks they got from waiters and other patrons when they walked into the restaurant and all sat down together. I asked them to design a ritual that would honor their experience, to prepare a domestic eucharist with only one expectation: that they and their guests would all feel welcome and even comfortable there. I rejoiced at their creativity and the fact that they had indeed grasped a basic goal of the class: to uncover the hidden and often insidious structures of domination implicit in ritual and prayer. Not a single prayer was *for* their guests, who were addressed now as friends. Rather, they prayed *with* them for their well-being and their needs, anticipating a time when they might one day be praying *as* one of them, more accurately, *as one with* them.

"Give us this day our daily bread." "Bread" is the street word for money. Economic factors are critical aspects of contemporary concerns for justice. Give us, now, necessary "bread," essential "bread," "bread" for life's essentials. Years ago I prepared a biblical presentation for the Ministry of Money movement with which I have long been associated. I discovered, much to my amazement, that in the New Testament there are more references to money than just about anything else. Knowing this helped me to understand just how integral money is, not only to our material welfare, but to our spiritual well-being as well.

When asked to lead a weekend retreat for the movement's board of directors, I designed a domestic eucharist with money as the basic element. "In God we trust" is inscribed on all our nation's money as a stamp of integrity, yet we no longer believe that God has anything at all to do with our money and the way it is earned or spent. We no longer trust our money or trust ourselves with money, no longer trust there will be enough for everyone who needs it, for the times that we will need it to sustain and enjoy life. We have driven a wedge between money and God. We link one with greed and the Other with grace. We have pushed them to opposite extremes in our lives, then wonder why we find ourselves pulled in two directions, sometimes toward an evil empire, sometimes toward paradise. Money is associated with acquisition and with accumulation, not with giving away, which is why in a world where there is so much of it around, so little of it seems to get around to the places where it is most needed. What would it be like if we could change our perception of money? If only we could see money as something not just to have and to hold for ourselves, but as resource to benefit others, a means of eliminating the inexcusable inequities in the world.

As one small step in this direction, I filled a basket with money — coins and bills of different denominations, not a whole lot because it was mine and I am anything but wealthy. Before the close of the ritual, as an expression of communion, we passed the basket around the circle. In a spirit of thanksgiving, each of us took money out instead of putting it in. I asked them to add to the amount they had taken and to use that money to do some good, either through a random act of kindness or a contribution to a cause they ordinarily would not have supported. Be some-what serendipitous, I said. Let it lead to some new awareness. I asked them to send me a postcard telling me what they did. I was surprised by the degree of consideration that preceded the deeds that were done. Our world could use more of that. It was amaz-ing to see how new levels of discovery happened even to those whose consciousness had already been raised. None of us who participated will ever again think of the word "bread," or perhaps even "eucharist," in quite the same way.

Significant within all our bread-breaking traditions is the pres-ence of the Holy Spirit — God's spirit, the spirit of Jesus — and that aspect of transformation that leaves us in some way changed.

Whether or not our theology speaks of symbol or sign or substance, the realization that God-with-us is present here within us is the essence of our efforts to describe what we mean by real — the Real Presence of the living God. Today, in continuity with the earliest of our traditions, we call upon the Holy Spirit to transform our eucharistic community, so that we might continue undeterred in our desire to embrace the spirit of Jesus in memory of him.

Come, O Holy Spirit, enter the hearts of all who crave communion with each other, whether through word or sacrament, through sacramental Eucharist or sacramental meal. May all who break bread, through God's grace, in some way be transformed. That means, may we be changed — substantively, substantially — so we are no longer the way we were, and although the same, are not the same. May it be said, may it be so, that beneath our outward appearance, we are vehicles of grace. We are embodied Spirit. We are one with one another. We are one with God.

> *What do You ask of me?*
> *What would You have me do?*
> *I give myself within*
> *these gifts I offer You.*
> *This bread is food for life.*
> *This wine is spirit of love*
> *for You.*
>
> *What can I offer You?*
> *You've given life to me.*
> *You're part of all I am.*
> *What would You have me be?*
> *This bread is food for life.*
> *This wine is spirit of love*
> *for me.*

Feed Me, Fill Me

I have never experienced a tornado, thank God, but those who have say that it sounds like a runaway freight train bellowing its intent to blow the world to bits. Was that what Pentecost was like? Was the sound of that very violent wind filling the house where the faithful were gathered as devastating as a tornado? Was the Holy Spirit a destructive whirlwind forcing people to reconstruct their religious lives from the bottom up? From what we know of that moment and its aftermath, that seems to have been the case.

The Spirit of God is no nesting dove. Where God's Spirit is, there is chaos. We need to understand that about the Spirit in our lives. Sometimes the chaos is called to order as it was in the beginning in the story of creation according to Genesis. At other times complacency erupts into chaotic confusion, as in the blowout at Pentecost, unraveling everything. We need reminding from time to time that the Holy Spirit is the vital force of God's abiding presence in that chaos within us and around us. Wind, therefore, is an apt image of the Spirit's graced initiatives. Its many moods reflect that unbounded, originating energy that blows where it will.

The wind of the Spirit danced through the church and blew away centuries of accretion when windows onto a wider world

were thrown open at Vatican II. Every now and then we feel
the unrelenting demands of divinity breaking into those cramped
rooms where our hesitant hearts are hiding, pushing against our
rigidities, dismantling our false securities, destroying prejudicial
ideologies, shaking loose our stranglehold on religion and theology. The Spirit can appear as frightening as a storm or as
comforting as a mother's breath, that warm caress on a baby's
skin assuring us all is well.

I have felt the wind of the Spirit blow so many times in so
many places. Now and then it hits with Pentecost force in an unexpected insight. For example, the time I suddenly realized that
the upper room at Pentecost had to be filled with women. Conditioned nearly all of my life by images and homilies insisting that
twelve tiny tongues of flame hovered over twelve bearded men, I
missed the fact that Scripture itself quietly disputes that claim.

When I close my eyes I can see them there, a multitude of
women, all those who had been touched by Jesus and irrevocably
transformed, either physically or spiritually, liberated from sub-
servience, free at last to be themselves, to take chances, to make
choices.

I believe it was and continues to be a truly egalitarian Pentecost, God's Spirit poured out in abundance on young and old,
slave and free, on women as well as men. I believe they were
there together, women as well as men, when they felt the full
force of the Spirit like a mega-hurricane shaking their souls and
spirits to the very foundations of their being, women as well as
men. I believe they were caught up in the Spirit as if in a heavenly rapture, women as well as men; that they felt the Spirit burn
like a raging fire deep within them, women as well as men; that
they burst from the room to tell the world about what they were
experiencing, women as well as men; that their feelings had not
yet found the words so that they could only babble and stam-
mer about faith and new life and beginning again, women as well
as men; that many who heard them felt the fire and a similar

stirring within them and were able to comprehend their illiterate speech in that place within that is beyond words, translating into their own life experience the testimony of God's miraculous ways within women as well as men.

It is forever Pentecost. We seem to prefer that upper room of rationality and cognition, prefer to remain locked into set ways that are essentially of our own making, fearful of relinquishing whatever it is on which we are religiously dependent, women as well as men. The Spirit knows where to find us and precisely how to reach us, and does so, again and again, blowing to bits our presuppositions, creating chaos around us and within us, opening a path for preparing a radically new creation in the church and in the world.

We must learn to embrace the chaos of our times as the potential for re-creation, learn to welcome the fire within, no matter how much it burns. We must dare to tell what we have seen and heard when visited by the Spirit, to speak of our experience courageously in public places, no matter what the cost. If this frightens us and others, so be it, for this I really do believe, that "it is God in Christ who has commissioned us, who has put a seal upon us and given us the Spirit in our hearts as a guarantee" (2 Cor. 1:21–22). God's "guarantee" will surely guide us and safeguard our fidelity.

I have been blessed with an abiding awareness of the Spirit in my life, knowing intensely the truth of this in ways I find hard to express except through metaphor. So often Spirit's indwelling presence whispers in what I say or sing, giving not only words but also images and insight. Daily I feel the guiding force of Spirit within and around me, pushing me, pulling me, dancing with me toward some unseen horizon through the maze of earthbound, planetary energy pulsating throughout the here and now that I so dearly love. How do I know it is Spirit? How do we know we're in love except through the love we feel so passionately that we become the love we receive and give, for beloved and love are one. I feel the Spirit in my spirit, in my belly, my bones, the whole of my being, in all that I see and touch. Spirit is everywhere. The old separations of this from that no longer have any meaning, for in Spirit's world, all spirit is one. There is something so innately freeing about this inchoate yet growing sensitivity to a oneness with the inner spirit of all living things. It helps me to hear the music, the fetal heartbeat of the new creation in the womb of planet earth and in the cosmic expanse of galaxies beyond innumerable galaxies. Spirit is the soul of the universe out there and in me.

If only awareness were constant and sabbath space unending, but there is always Monday morning when the harsh light of reality shows us who we are. That is when Spirit really kicks in. Here is a good example. I invited a friend and colleague to teach in a program I direct, the Women's Leadership Institute. When she was finished we stood and talked and she spotted the tote bag on my shoulder, which was full of books and papers. "I want that bag. It has my colors." She's refreshingly direct. When I hesitated, she persisted. "Give me that bag. I've got to have it." Now why didn't I just give it to her? Those were her colors. She was my friend. She had made a sincere request. Part of me said she should have it, but for reasons I find hard to understand, I did not want to do it. Suddenly, I was saying to myself, I like this bag. I want to keep it. It evokes good memories. Presbyterian women gave it to me when I addressed six thousand of them last summer. It's just the right size, it holds all my books, and yes, it has great colors, my favorite colors too. I heard her say, "Don't do it, if it really means something special to you," but I said I would, and eventually did, but not until the following morning. Now why, I asked myself over and over, did I respond like that? Insensitively and selfishly and so reluctantly. Why was I clinging to a cloth bag? Its symbolic value had already shifted. It had now become a painful reminder to me of my holding back, of a flaw in the keeping of my vow to steer clear of excessive attachments, of something in me that had cast a shadow I really did not want to see.

A week later a package arrived for me from a former student. I opened it up and pulled out a bag, a cloth bag, a big cloth bag, even bigger than the one I had given away, with a design and colors that were made for me: a beautifully embroidered planet earth with children of the world holding hands and holding up the planet. The children seemed to be singing. On the outside of the bag was a pouch pocket that held several papers. One was a map of Cape Cod on the coast of Massachusetts with a circle around a seaside town and arrows leading to it. The other was a note from my friend Jean, saying, "Here is our new home overlooking the water. Come anytime. It is your home too. There's a room set aside just for you. The key is in the pocket." Sure enough, there was the key, attached to a tiny blue plastic container filled with sand and sea water and a very small shell.

Such are the ways of the Spirit in my life, responding to my struggle for fidelity with infinite compassion, generosity, serendipity, and humor. A bag for a bag, and then some. Coincidence? Indeed it was, but in my vocabulary, coincidence is a sacred word, the calling card of the Spirit. Such incidents of harmonic convergence are tokens of love from a loving God whose Spirit reveals this to me. It isn't always easy to integrate the lessons learned from experience. For example, I recall a moment in time when I stood in a camp of refugees who had nothing at all but the clothes on their back, and even those were ragged. I thought, as soon as I get back home, I'll take the clothes from my closet and those that are stuffed in dresser drawers and give them all away. Now that memory is joined by another. Here I am back home again in the midst of an affluent culture, clinging to my cloth bag. How long will it take to learn what it means to carry too much baggage? Perhaps I'm a little wiser now. When I opened the gift from Jean, I heard myself say, "I love this bag," and suddenly, I remembered. So I paused, prayed, and in my heart, prepared to

let it go. As for the house by the side of the sea, now that's a
little different. I smiled as I put the key in my desk. One step at
a time, please, Spirit. One small step at a time.

Ours is a generation of seekers. One source of common wisdom says that you find only what you are looking for. Another
insists that if you try too hard to find a certain thing — like love,
security, even happiness — it will almost always elude you. So
what are we looking for? People I know are searching for a deeper
spiritual connection, a deeper understanding of that which is unseen, that which we call Spirit. We want to feel the Spirit, feel
that fire in the belly that is a sure sign of the Spirit in our lives.

Where do we go to get the Spirit? For those who seek the
Spirit, that is the wrong question. It sends the seeker too far
afield. We do not need to go anywhere, for the Spirit is all around
us and down deep beneath the skin of all living things. Besides,
nobody gets the Spirit. The Spirit gets us. Still, there is a world
of indifference between saying that the Spirit inhabits our heart
and feeling the fire within. And so we go on searching, looking
for ways to bridge the gap between interpreting Spirit and being
in the Spirit, between theological discourse and the rapture of a
moment that is truly Spirit-inspired.

Any successful search begins with the right focus question. It
puts us on the appropriate path, allows us to narrow our options
to what is most relevant. The question that needs to be asked is
this: how can we become more acutely aware of the God-given
gift of Spirit that is already ours, so that our lives are truly Spirit-
defined and our actions Spirit-led?

We could use a little help from tradition and a whole lot more
from that wholly revealing Spirit who may seem to us elusive
yet is so eager to be found. Religion has had the upper hand in
communicating Spirit throughout Christian tradition, designating media that mediate Spirit: sacred Scripture, our sacramental
rites, dogmas and decisions of the magisterium for those who are
Roman Catholic, the words of priests and prophets, our sages and

our saints. It has always been understood that once one got religion, one had all the essential tools for accessing the Holy Spirit, that no further search was necessary. Just do it and it will deliver. This assumption has stood the test of time, but in the paradigm shifts of our century, its basis has come undone.

Clearly, there have always been individuals who have felt free to follow a path of their own in and out of religion, and there have always been charismatic communities caught up in a Pentecostal fervor. The same is also true today, but something else is emerging, a movement of epic proportions that is threatening institutional religion's uncontested control of the Spirit in our lives. Discerning women and men are saying that they have felt the Spirit, but it has not been at designated times or in designated places, and certainly not in prescribed patterns or in predetermined ways. Many are also saying that they have found a stifling of spirit in the institutional church, where childhood credos seldom mature, where there is a lack of sympathy for a sincere wrestling with how faith functions in the complexities of daily life. A systematic theology and a rigidly regulated ritual response are no longer enough for a growing number of dedicated Christians who long to live with integrity. Many feel caught in a tug-of-war between ecclesiastical mandates and a desire to follow in the spirit of Jesus, wherever that may lead.

The result has been that many, particularly women, have begun to take responsibility for their own spiritual lives. All around the world today individuals dare to speak the names of the God of their experience, articulating alone and in the company of others prayers of supplication and invocations of praise. They are standing in solidarity with those traditionally outside the circle drawn by patriarchal privilege and are nourishing their newly evolving selves with alternative liturgies. They feel they are drawn to do what they do by the Spirit of that very tradition that has kept Spirit contained, calling to life a more ancient response inherent in authorized liturgy and in authoritative texts.

This phenomenon of a church of the Spirit is not in competition with nor meant as a public condemnation of the institution within which it coexists, although it is quick to critique that institution. Born of a desire for a just church, it is gift of the Spirit in troublesome times, a visible incentive to hold fast to hope, a tangible witness to that which religion itself can aspire to become. The Spirit church believes it is the very soul of the institution and has no intention of severing such an integral relationship, for the ties that bind are strong and deep and a love for one's tradition, with all of its limitations and flaws, continues to live on.

We who would live by the Spirit require special gifts of the Spirit to survive the tests of time. Among these are courage and tenacity, for it is not easy to embrace the Spirit in the midst of conflicting claims. We who look to the Just One for a truly transformed society know the extent of the wilderness that lies between us and the promised land. As gestation time for a just church moves through yet another century, all who labor to bring it about cry out once again, How long? God alone knows when or even if these birth pangs will ever end. Yet not all prophets have been silenced, nor is every dream stillborn. A life force is still viable, a vision still discernible, vitality still welling up and spilling forth from the body of the church, and for this we give thanks to God. As we leave the terrible twos to embrace a third millennium, we pray that in our growing diversity of style and form and substance we may remember that we are a body of many parts but only one Spirit. We pray as we cross the threshold into a whole new era that we may all be of one spirit and our hearts of one accord.

> *Spirit of God, Spirit of God, Spirit of God, feed me, fill me.*
> *Spirit of God, Spirit of God, Spirit of God, feed me, fill me.*
> *Spirit of God, Spirit of God, Spirit of Goodness, feed me.*
> *Spirit of God, Spirit of God, Spirit of Goodness, fill me.*

So You came, sowing seeds,
knowing my name, knowing my needs . . .
feed me . . . fill me.

Come and sow deep in me
seasons to grow, reason to be . . .
feed me . . . fill me.

Spirit-fire, bearer of
all I desire, all of my love . . .
feed me . . . fill me.

Spirit of God, Spirit of God, Spirit of God, feed me, fill me.
Spirit of God, Spirit of God, Spirit of God, feed me, fill me.
Spirit of God, Spirit of God, Spirit of Goodness, feed me.
Spirit of God, Spirit of God, Spirit of Goodness, fill me.

A New Path

It was a Saturday in October of 1994. There was nothing unusual about the day, except for the fact that I was at home with a bit of time on my hands. I was quietly clearing up some things when all of a sudden, with no prior warning, I had an anxiety attack, a severe existential panic that triggered a trembling inside and out. This had never happened to me before. I did not know how to deal with it. I sat down, got up, began to cry, walked around and around the room and up and down the stairs, then started to talk to myself out loud, hoping to analyze the cause so I could take control again, so I could get a grip on myself, so it would go away. It lasted approximately ten minutes, then stopped as it had started, as though someone had pulled a plug. I was as I had been before, as if it had never happened, except that I was badly shaken. I shared the episode with my assistant at work the following Monday. She said the same thing had happened to her, only ten minutes earlier. We sat there in amazement, then together we both said, "Pika!"

Our Native American friend whose name means Shadow Basket had said she was going on a vision quest to discern our spirit names. I had forgotten all about it. She had not told us when this would be. I called her and, yes, it happened on Saturday. At the very time that I was so distressed, she said that she had connected with me, had entered my mind, was discerning my spirit. She said she had a new name for me, that she had had a vision, a dream, and this is what she saw. Her dream was about me. I am in the middle of nowhere, knee-deep in dead leaves. There is no path. No one knows how to proceed. Suddenly, I produce a sacred broom and I start sweeping. A path is revealed. Only I know where the path is. I continue going forward. She told me my name is *Ché etíin* in Navajo — Pathfinder — that I had always been a pathfinder. I thanked her for her gift to me and prayed that I would live into and up to my new name.

I may well be a pioneer following paths that lead to the edge and sometimes moving beyond them, but this has not always been obvious, especially to me, and it has not always been true. As a child, as an adolescent, I never strayed outside the lines but adhered to rules that defined for me the leeway and the limits. In school, in church, on the social scene I did what I was expected to do and for that I was rewarded. I may have communed with the God of my spirit through metaphors and imagination, but the God of my religious life up to the time of Vatican II had to endure my strict conformity and words I repeated by rote. The girlhood gifts I gave consisted of Masses, novenas, and rosaries, not just a few, but dozens, sometimes even a hundred or more that I would list on a handmade card. I never did know what my mother really thought when I gave her a card for Mother's Day with fifty thousand ejaculations!

Since God sees through to the inside of people and the Spirit directs from within, I was drawn to a community that would take me beyond my limitations to the outer edge of my circumscribed world, and I embraced the call. It is in this context that I grew to understand the value of pushing the limits in certain situations and the necessity at times of breaking the rules to accomplish a greater good. The community had experienced this in the circumstances of its founding. Canon law prohibited those with religious vows in the church to practice medicine in its full scope. Anna Dengel, a female physician with experience in India, wanted to promote Catholic medical missions in an area of dire need through a full array of medical services with hospitals and physicians, and she wanted to make this available within the context of vowed religious life. She was forbidden to do so, but the Spirit showed the way where there seemed to be no way. With several other women, she established a community with no canonical standing, no official recognition, no means of support whatever except for the generosity of others. The need was great and the professional and dedicated service of the sisters made a difference and an impact. The fledgling community was so effective the church changed canon law. Anna Dengel recalls this in her own words in *The Medical Missionary* in 1955, the year I entered the community:

> Anyhow in spite of the different weathers we had to brave on our maiden voyage into a new field, we can honestly say that the winds were favorable to us. Eleven years after our foundation, Rome confirmed the "Holy Experiment." On February 11, 1936, the Sacred Congregation of Propaganda Fide in the Instruction *Constans ac Sedula* approved of the study and practice of medicine for mission sisters with public vows. (September–October, p. 127)

I caught the pioneer spirit during my integration into this international, cross-cultural society. It grew to become an integral part of me and my ministry.

There is a card I keep in my office that says: "You cannot discover new oceans unless you have the courage to lose sight of the shore." That may be what drew me intuitively to seek out situations of risk. An occasional companion of risk is the element of fear. I can recall several different times when I had moved a bit too far afield and experienced genuine fear.

On my return to Thailand in 1984, I joined Dee, a physician friend, and crossed over into Cambodia without authorization.

Dee had accepted responsibility for meeting the basic medical needs of Khmer Rouge soldiers, the very ones who had implemented a four-year reign of terror that culminated in the death of several million Cambodian people. Overthrown by the military of Vietnam, they were now dispersed in disillusioned groups in the jungle along the border. I will never forget the stone-cold stares, eyes boring into me from the men who were in that isolated camp in a small, sunless clearing miles from anywhere. I met the leader of the camp, a small, unassuming woman who, Dee had informed me, had been personally responsible for the deaths of approximately seventy thousand people. I had ministered to some of the survivors several years before. So that's what unadulterated evil looks like. The thought frightened me even more when I realized that it looks human, just like me.

The following year in Ethiopia, as we were setting up our center for emaciated children, another incident occurred that left me feeling weak in the knees. We had outgrown the grass hut and were on our way to the village school about a mile down the road. We were told we could use the three small rooms enclosed within the compound because school was not in session. It would have been an easy walk if our arms weren't full of children, and if those who could walk were not so weak, and if the long-awaited rains could have waited a little longer. I lost my boot every time my foot stepped into the black clay mud. We have to walk on the road, I said, a narrow strip of pavement that stretched forever in both directions to link us to places unknown. Maura went to turn the truck around so she could transport our supplies. Make sure you stay on the road, I shouted, which would be quite a challenge, for the width of the road was approximately equal to the width of our truck. Maura was a wee wisp of a thing, a nurse from Ireland. She had spent years in situations such as this, and she revved the truck with gusto. I hoped there would be no traffic for there was room for only one, but since we hadn't seen a vehicle in hours, the chances were remote. Instinctively, I glanced up the road and much to my horror saw a long line of military trucks approaching from a distance.

As the line drew closer I could tell that it stretched as far as the eye could see. "Hurry up, Maura, there's a convoy coming, and for God's sake, please don't stall." She was into her sixth maneuver of inching forward and slipping back, when, wouldn't you know, the engine coughed and I heard the sound of silence. The long olive line approached, slowed, and came to a screeching halt, as a regiment of horns blared into infinity. I felt like it took her a week and a half before she got that truck in gear and heading in the right direction. When Maura drove off, I stood there, silently, defiantly, with a skeletal child held tight in my arms and rain falling on my head as more than one hundred trucks passed by. One by one, the drivers of all the vehicles, who looked to me like Khmer Rouge military, for they were ethnically Asian, turned toward me as they approached and stabbed me with their eyes. I died one hundred times that day wondering which of the vehicles would finally decide to shoot. In the back of each of the open trucks were approximately twenty soldiers, all Ethiopians. When they saw two white women, for Carolyn had remained with me, standing there in the pouring rain surrounded by starving children, they began throwing small wrapped sweets to where the kids could reach them. Not too many had strength enough to reach out very far. God bless you, I whispered, again and again, as the rain ran down my quivering face, rain and a river of tears.

When I think of fear I remember that afternoon in a game park in Kenya as the day was drawing to a close. You had to be out of the park before dark for a whole list of reasons, all of which spelled danger. We were on our way to one of the gates when I saw the perfect photo, a variety of animals grazing at the edge of a lake that was red-rimmed in the setting sun. I persuaded Janet to get a bit closer, for she was behind the wheel and I was in charge of the camera. We drove closer and still a bit closer and then we were immobile, up to our four-wheel hubcaps in notorious African mud. Every spin of the wheel dug our dilemma deeper. We were far from the exits, miles from help, feeling absolutely helpless and, to be honest, a little scared. Suddenly, we heard in the distance the reverberation of men's voices. My stomach sank when I saw the truck, a large pickup open in back and jammed with roughly fifty men, all whooping and hollering in a language I did not understand, hollering to Janet and me. My heart beat wildly, my skin froze, my knees began to buckle. Was this our deliverance or our demise? There we were, two lone females, stuck in the mud, trapped by a lake in an isolated area of the park as darkness was descending.

The truck headed straight to us. Janet, calm but determined, a length of tow rope in her hand, walked to where the truck had stopped and greeted them in Swahili. It helped that she knew their language. It did not hurt that she wore a veil, for we still wear veils in Kenya. A discussion ensued that soon shifted to what sounded like an argument. A dozen men were shouting. I could tell that they were really mad. What's going on, I asked her, certain that she had pleaded for our lives and was on the verge of losing. "I asked them to pull us out," she said. "I showed them the rope, they said okay, but they are asking for too much money." "How much?" I asked. "Do we have enough?" "Oh, yes," she assured me, "but it isn't fair. I'm not going to pay them." I couldn't believe my ears. Suddenly, I felt dizzy, felt like I was going to faint as a wave of relief hit smack against the ludicrousness of her decision. "Give them the stupid money," I shouted. "Do you want us to stay here all night?" Once the financial affairs had been settled, we were out of there with a pull and a push with all of those hands to assist us, but not before getting a lecture about how dumb we were, leaving the road as night approached and getting stuck in the mud. Let me tell you, they got that right.

There are consequences to breaking rules, some more acute than others, even with regard to religion, especially regarding religion, whether in matters of rites or rubrics, dogma or theology. When I first began to question the legitimacy of one or more long-held beliefs like, you will burn in hell if you don't go to Mass on Sunday, or, it is the will of God and the intention of Jesus that the priesthood should be closed to women, I felt a response akin to fear catch hold of me for an instant. This was followed by an onslaught of should and ought and guilt and must, a long line of soldiers, indecipherable din from the back of a truck giving rise to anxiety, seeking to assert control over me, determined to keep me in line. Faith had always meant keeping the rules. That's how faith was measured, by the extent of our fidelity to a raft of regulations. God was a fierce taskmaster. So I was told, so I was taught, though my heart knew otherwise. Patriarchy's domineering "power over" is a fierce deterrent to freedom of will and beastly to overcome. Residual effects may linger for years, long after the mind has acquiesced to a more wholistic sense of God, one rooted in love, not law, in compassion, not intimidation.

It is critically important that we shift the emphasis from fear to freedom, from guilt to delight, from obligation to anticipation when it comes to ourselves and the All-holy One, if we would end that tug-of-war between common sense and a captive conscience. It took a while until I was pulled far enough into the changing paradigm to identify with it. What helped was to know I was not alone. Far from it, as I discovered in my pilgrimage around the world and into the homes and hearts of those who are seeking to live with integrity and to pray authentically. Our numbers now are legion. What also helped was to have a solid spiritual and theological basis to accompany all the changes that were burgeoning around me and in me. God's Spirit provided continuity. A new understanding of Jesus convinced me to stay the course.

Jesus left the world like he entered it, breaking all the rules. Miracles accompanied his birth and his death, miracles witnessed by women and experienced directly and intimately by women, yet then, as now, no matter how valid that experience, the men would not believe them. Men, not all, and fewer every year, but still an overwhelming number, do not believe what women see or say or know or experience. It has always been the other way around for countless generations: men speak and men interpret and women have believed them. Fortunately, that is changing.

Blessed are you who see and believe. This is a word of good news for women and a growing number of men. Believe what you see, what the Spirit reveals, what your searching heart envisions, and trust your experience. We must begin to believe in ourselves and the wisdom inherent within us. Internalized negative messages limit the Spirit's power to revitalize and make new. Every time we feel liberated within and nurtured by the hope that sustains us, we witness to the plenitude of grace on behalf of those who are pushed to the margins of opportunity and power. All who have experienced the God of the oppressed making a way where there is no way within the institution want to shout the good news from the housetops. Women keep silent in the church? Not when such things are happening in our hearts and spirits and psyches. We will, we must share this good news with others, even if nobody believes us.

The trend within the hierarchy to silence unnotarized speech is contrary not only to common sense but to the signs of the times we live in. One can only wonder, is the speech of the masses so cogent, so convincing, that silencing millions and millions of voices seems the only alternative? One must ask yet another question. Is protecting a tradition, any tradition, worth the intrinsic violence implicit in so extreme an action? The freedom to speak, to enter into dialogue or scholarly debate or to share opinions openly and honestly is a fundamental human value that distinguishes a free society from a politically oppressive regime. Those of us who live under the vow or within the spirit of obedience know that being subject to authority means we have every word but the last.

While many are seeking to find their footing on a new path through tradition, those in the church who are charged with responsibility for providing direction are frantically trying to re-discover a path left long ago. There is a lingering nostalgia among some cradle Catholics to recover the ethos of a time when all of us knew what it meant to be Catholic: everyone everywhere the same, a singular witness to the world beyond the world we had constructed, the only world we knew. There is only one way to be Catholic, right? Not any longer. Not today. That's where times have changed.

We are told that the underlying issue is the loss of a sense of community. The issue, however, is not lack of community, but rather how one defines it. The uniformity of conformity is not this generation's conceptualization of *koinonia*. At least we know what that word convokes. Wait a few more years and no one will even comprehend it. Today new forms of community are spring-ing up everywhere. The individual's need for others is affirmed by the value of coming together and celebrating common cause. The small group phenomenon is sweeping the country and flourishing beyond our borders. Postconciliar Catholics and feminist Chris-tians are at the heart of this trend. There is an abundance of graced initiatives in and beyond the institutional church reflect-ing a vitality of spirit that is unmistakably community. The hope that we might once again rally around the way we were is well intentioned but unrealistic. The demographics of contemporary Catholicism reveal that a majority of the faithful are offspring of the spirit and the dynamics of Vatican II. We speak a different language, are shaped by a new understanding, and no longer hold blind obedience to be quintessential to fidelity. It is critical that church leadership, whatever the denomination, make an effort to come into the present if we are to have a future church.

Community today can be understood only from the perspec-tive of diverse cultures and, yes, individuality, for individuals matter. God loves each of us unconditionally and holds us all accountable, not en masse, but one by one. We have a lot we can teach one another about the essence of community, not theoretically, but from experience. Those who have known the blessing of an affirming, empowering community can only be satisfied in a welcoming place where everybody knows your name, your strengths, your weaknesses, and loves you anyway. True community means communion on a level that is deep and transforming, the linking of disparate spirits in a commitment to uphold the common good within and beyond that entity gathered together for prayer and praise. Different communities do things differently according to the gifts and intuitive spirit of culture, gender, age. This may well be the hardest lesson for the institution to learn. The challenge for future generations will be the integration of unlimited diversity into all aspects of our life, and that challenge is already here. It is a mystery to me why institutional religion expends so much time and energy ensuring that we look and act alike and that everything stays the same. The movement of the Spirit is toward pluriformity. True community is expected to find its unity within that frame.

On my desk, I keep another card with a motivational saying. "Do not follow where the path may lead....Go instead where there is no path and leave a trail." Two paths diverged. I happened to take the one that was less traveled at the time. Many others are doing the same.

Come, Sophia, Holy Wisdom, gateway to eternity.
Sacred source of all that is from long before earth came to be.
In Your womb the primal waters from below and from above
gently rock Your sons and daughters, born to wisdom and to love.

Come, Sophia, be a clear compelling presence everywhere.
Still the terror, dry the tears, come, ease the burdens that we bear.
From the first faint light of morning, through the dark when day is done,
be the midwife of our borning and the rising of our sun.

Come, Sophia, intuition weaving wisdom deep within,
bringing promise to fruition through the prophets that have been,
pleading justice for tomorrow and forgiveness for today
for the images we borrow and the roles we often play.

Come, Sophia, we believe You are the shaman of the soul.
Break us open to receive You; fill us up and make us whole.
You inspire us to envision all the fullness of shalom
on a new path through tradition that will surely lead us home.

Our Many Paths

I left Connecticut in mid-January of the snowiest winter on record and disembarked into the heat of Bombay, where a whole new world caught hold of me. New sights. New sounds. New spiritualities. Clutter, clatter, and above all people, more people than one can imagine could fit into a territory of that size.

My community had been founded to bring Catholic medical missions to India in the form of hospitals, clinics, nursing schools, and a variety of training programs designed to engage the local people in what we were about, to raise the standard of professional medicine, and to work ourselves out of a job. In the hospitals that we built and staffed, the whole family was welcome, as patients and as visitors, and our mission spread to other countries and other continents. A particular focus in India was the Muslim woman denied medical care because of the religious custom of purdah, which meant she could be seen only by those men who were in her immediate family. Our hospitals set aside areas exclusively for women and provided female physicians. Women of all religious persuasions were admitted as patients and as students in our schools of nursing. What flourished in the wake of this endeavor were indigenous vocations. Today Indian sisters represent the largest cultural group in our community, making up more than one-third of our membership and providing pioneering leadership locally and worldwide.

I went to India to experience India — its culture, its religions, its diversity, and its indigenous liturgy — and to learn how Indian women were faring in terms of development. But I also went primarily to meet face to face the many Indian sisters I knew only secondhand, whose names appeared on letters and cards and in congregational reports, women who had been singing my songs faithfully ever since their inception and whose love and support have meant so much to me for so many years.

I traveled throughout India by bus, train, plane, on foot, and in three-wheeled auto rickshaws, moving in and out of numerous subcultures, each with a language and dialects, distinctive customs and cuisine that characterize the various provinces and diverse demographic regions of this pluralistic land. India is a subcontinent of contrasts, of luxuriant tropics and bonedry deserts, of sun-drenched beaches and snowcapped peaks, of teeming cities and remote villages, of tribal and national identities, of religions and their ritual realities, of wealth and debilitating poverty, of opportunity and the lack of it, of life defined from birth to death by the implications of caste. It is also a land of incredible beauty made manifest in so many ways, of intoxicating music that seeps into the soul and psyche until one is one with the song. It is a land where God feels at home and folk feel at home with God.

Among my cherished memories are the village and tribal peoples whom I met along the way; dedicated women and men in urban and rural settings whose life work was oriented toward helping those in need; the fisherfolk of South India who are struggling for survival as they try to eke out a living from the dredges of the sea; the Mothers' Union in West Garo Hills, a grassroots cooperative of several hundred women from a number of villages who came together to meet with me because I care about women, singing, dancing, garlanding me, and sharing their hopes for a future more promising than the past. How delighted I was to discover that women's cooperatives, self-help groups, and focused feminist initiatives are springing up everywhere, that there were 88,000 women's organizations in Maharashtra province alone. And just before I left, on International Women's Day in Ranchi, the capital of southern Bihar, I watched thousands of tribal women march for fundamental human rights for themselves and for their children.

I visited ancient temple caves and the sacred site of Bodghaya to be touched by the spirit of the Buddha, mingled with Hindu pilgrims seeking sunrise on the Ganges in Varanasi (also known as Banaras) to witness the strength of their faith in their prayer offerings. I saw Christianity's Eastern face in rich ritual expressions rooted in an Indian way of life. I will never again underestimate the integrating power of a truly indigenous liturgy, something we in America have yet to understand.

India lives now deep inside where the heart stores its treasures and entrusts them to memory. Such memories grow more precious with time. To share them is to celebrate life and to feast upon recall. I kept a poetry journal, a sampling of experiences encoded in verse and metaphor. These intuitive reflections on what I felt about what I saw and heard preserve for me more accurately than prose those graced events and encounters. I would like to share some of them with you. Here is a glimpse into my journal.

Pune, my first stop, a bustling city four hours southeast of Bombay by bus.

Silently
in the predawn dark
one
lone
tin-faced façade
opens
a corrugated eye
and from the belly
of raw routine
steps
a woman,
sari-clad,
to sweep a semicircle clear
of destitution
and debris,
brave alternative
in a sea
of litter
and illiteracy.

Daily prayer, silent or celebratory in the form of indigenous liturgy at the chapel of the Medical Mission Sisters in Pune.

Little lamp,
light
the wick
of my heart,
quicken
my capacity
for prayer,
ignite
the oil of my soul's
solitude
that I too
in this interlude
might dance
around
a mandala
of flowers
designating
this place
holy ground,
site of profound
and hidden powers.

Atman
Allah
Adonai
I worship You
through all
in all
and garland You
with songs of praise
honoring
the ancient ways
of Bible
Qur'an
Upanishad
on my soul's journey
into God.

Kottayam, the capital city in the lush southern province of Kerala.

The raucous
caw caw
caucus
of crows
crescendoes
to a deafening din
as the congregation
settles in
to serenade
the setting sun
and call up the moon
when day is done.
Here in India
crows are gray.
They are black
back in the USA,
yet congregate
the same way
to roost
or nest
day after day.
East
and west
share common cause
through nature's laws.
The gap between
disintegrates
through this routine.

Everywhere
crows
cronies
crones
share in the ritual
earth intones.
Crows circle
overhead,
crows surround
my borrowed bed,
and I am
strangely
comforted.

The beach at Kanniyakumari in Tamil Nadu, the southernmost tip of India, at the point where three oceans meet: the Arabian Sea, the Indian Ocean, and the Bay of Bengal.

The sun
overslept
in a bed of cloud.
The waking world
began to pray.
A full moon
witnessed
the delay.
We watched for gold,
were given gray,
then the wind
blew us all away.
Like crows
we rose
in a thermal gust
and ventured forth
on wings of trust.
Cloud of Unknowing,
You are the One
we know and name
our Rising Sun.
Rise up
and stay
to light the way.
It is such
a roller coaster
day.

On the train to Trivandrum, also known as Thiruvananthapuram, in southern India.

God's love
flows into me
and through me
into the world.
These words,
the train,
a rocking refrain,
center me
rhythmically,
enter me
mystically,
as I sink
into
Mystery,
encounter
Divine
Density,
reach for
Infinite
Immensity,
embrace
Intuitive
Intensity.
Love
Love
grow in me,
go with me,
flow through me
and out
into
Your world.

Kerala in South India has some of the most beautiful beaches and sunsets anywhere in the world.

Kerala:
coconut palms
and husks,
rosewater dawns,
indigo dusks,
bluegreen seas,
sungold sand
lacing
the beaches embracing
the land
like bangles crafted
by God's hand.

The village of Poothura, which nestles between a river and the sea, is so beautiful but its people, fisherfolk of South India, are so poor.

A slip
of land,
a strip
of sand
between the river
and the sea,
river of life,
an artery,
a rough-hewn boat
transporting me
on backwaters
of a pulsating sea
into the heart
of Mystery:
paradise
poverty
paradox
doxology.

A liturgy led by the student nurses, welcoming me to Holy Family Hospital in Patna and held in Anna Dengel Hall, named in honor of the woman who founded the Medical Mission Sisters in 1925.

We dance
into the liturgy
led by women
of different castes
and diverse tribal cultures
wearing white
sulwar kamise
and brilliant red dupita,
their long black hair
and coal black eyes
match the music,
mesmerize.

Welcome the stranger,
the Word proclaims,
and I am garlanded
beneath a portrait of Anna
who is radiant
and rejoicing.
Because of one woman,
so many women
achieve the impossible
and miracles occur.
Today
I celebrate liturgy
in memory
of her.

Anna gave birth
God's way,
overcoming caste, cult, creed
with compassion
and the healer's craft.
They said it was impossible,
but
Sarah
Hannah
Mary
Anna
laughed.

Patna, a sprawling city on the banks of the river Ganges, not far from the border of Nepal, consists of an old section with crowded markets and narrow lanes and a modern addition where the pace is fast and full of life.

Dirt
diesel
dust
debris,
the din
of horns,
a swelling sea
of people
traffic
smoke
smells
sellers
buyers
cooking fires
men everywhere
hanging out,
cows
oxen
milling about,
sheep
goats
dogs
pigs
bikes
carts
transport rigs,

cycle rickshaws
six abreast
aim, advance,
ignore the rest,
buses
filled to overflowing
inside
outside
up on top:
Patna
on the banks
of the Ganges
living life
to the full
nonstop.

On the road from Mandar to the village of Kasiadhi in a rural area of Bihar province.

I sat and watched
the day awake
from the front seat
of a trekker van
moving through corridors
of trees,
a maharani
under her canopies.
The road
ran along open fields
and reached
for the far horizon,
where village spirits
left a trace
of their delicate presence
everyplace
in wisps of cloud
and mists of lace.
With a jolt,
a town jumped
out of a field
and ricocheted
off my window shield.

A whole new world
came into view,
doing
what I could never do,
snapshots of life
that somehow I knew
I would always be
returning to
in memory
or in spirit.
We rode right into
the rising sun
whose daily ritual
had begun
with *arthi*
to the all-holy One.
Like the day,
I too begin
by drawing light
from without
within.

Soon after a multinational corporation began strip mining in Phusri,
a village near Kasiadhi in Bihar, gaping holes and hillocks of debris
permanently altered the environment, neighborhoods were uprooted,
family members were separated and sent to live in other areas, and
the village itself, even to its name on local maps, disappeared from the
face of the earth.

They ripped the heart
right out of the land,
stripped it bare
of its heritage,
erased a village,
displaced a people,
defaced an ancient culture
with a massive pile
of rock
and bile
that had vomited
to the surface.
Gone the trees
to which birds had flown,
paddies and fields
where seeds
were sown,
sacred spaces
all had known
and loved
for generations.

All that remains
is stone
upon stone
and a gaping hole
deep
and wide,
bearing witness
to this geocide.
Earth,
ravaged
to the core,
howls.
It is Phusri
weeping for
a lost past,
a lost people,
for Phusri
is no more.

Written in Calcutta in West Bengal to honor both Rabindranath Tagore, a renowned Bengali poet, and a favorite poem from his collection the "Gitanjali," which begins: "Have you not heard his silent steps? He comes, comes, ever comes."

Here
the Bengali
poet
and mystic
heard the "Gitanjali"
singing
in the silence
of his heart.
To me
as well
the Eternal Presence
comes
comes
ever comes.
In me
and through me
as well
the Spirit
blows
like wind
through a wooden flute
making melodies
that please
as my heart
hums
hums
ever hums.

For me
as well
the goodness
and greatness
of God
overflows
in words
that sound
the Word
and resound
in living
and life-giving
song
that so often comes
and helps me become
like the One
to Whom I belong.

*On seeing the wide, majestic Brahmaputra River in Guwahati in
Assam in Northeast India.*

Who were those civilizations,
people
of ancient histories,
poets
who probed your mysteries,
formulated
philosophies,
theologies,
theosophies
along your banks,
O Brahmaputra,
and joined with you
in spirit
as you flowed
into the Ganga
and merged
with the sea?
What of those generations
of devout
sons and daughters
who bathed
in your sacred waters,
the emanations,
incantations,
revelations,
inspirations
that shaped a spirituality
rooted
in rites of worship
to multiple manifestations
of Supreme Deity?

Did they imagine,
as do I,
that God gives the names
to know God by?

O River of Life,
Living Water,
Source of Blessing,
isn't it so:
to You
and in You
and through You
all
mortal waters flow?
I believe
that You receive
all
authentic devotion,
that we
small droplets
in rivers of faith
will all converge
and one day
merge
in Love's
all-encompassing
ocean.

123

In the village of Mendipathar in the East Garo Hills, Meghalaya, Northeast India, near the end of my three-month pilgrimage.

Hot winds wilt
my attitude,
play havoc
with my mind
and mood
and I grow restless,
lose the will
for standing firm
or sitting still.
The clothes I washed
have blown
bone dry
beneath a brilliant
cloudless sky,
and gusts
that dust
the hills and plains
no longer preach
refreshing rains.
My inner eye
goes wandering,
images home
where it is spring,
but I resist
remembering.
My journey's end
is drawing near.

Let me be
fully present here
this little while
that is left for me
to savor
this reality,
for all too soon
hot winds will blow
to kingdom come
this calm I know.
Today I pray
simplicity
will find some way
to stay
with me
as India's lasting
legacy.

On an evening walk in Mendipathar, it was hard to tell the fireflies from the stars, there were so many of both above, below, and all around me.

Fields
of fireflies,
a flickering mass
disco dancing
in the grass,
blinking,
winking
as I pass,
mirror image
of myriad stars
that light our landscape
from above,
are
to me
reminiscent of
the fire of faith,
a spark of hope,
the lamp of love.
No matter what
unbelievers say,
all our nights
hold some small ray
of meaning,
even when our lives
show only shades
of gray on gray.

When we reflect
and when we pray,
God will be with us,
come what may.
Look for signs,
for messengers
that light the path
and point the way.
This
fireflies
convey:
when night falls
and fire
flies,
the trumpet calls,
the dead arise,
glory shines,
a loud voice cries,
behold
the Rapture!
On that day
we will go
dancing
all the way.

A reflection that came after spending a quiet afternoon in the presence of the magnificent Taj Mahal in Agra and remembering the Buddhist temple, Boudha Na in Katmandu and the many cathedral churches.

The monuments
we build
to love,
whether of stone
or steel
or glass
or something
more ephemeral
in homage to,
in honor of
our deities
or memories,
say
to time,
this shall not pass,
this momentary
encounter with
eternity,
infinity.
Our lives seek meaning
from what was,
crave temples,
stupas,
mosques,
shrines,
cathedrals
and basilicas.

We need reminders
now and then
of how love will transform,
and when,
to know it
when it comes again.
Time distorts
what nourishes.
The love that was,
so seldom is.

The beauty of other peoples, the validity of other traditions, new ways of knowing and naming God: all this and so much more I have kept from my encounter with India. We have much to learn before this moment passes into history and the future now breaking in upon us brings challenges of its own. We need to learn how to live together in a pluralistic world. We need to learn how to love each other and to accept that the One Who created us all responds to diverse rituals and to a variety of names.

We praise You, God of all the earth,
and all Your ways we bless.
In You all love begins and ends.
Your universal love transcends
our own dividedness.

We call to You with words we clothe
in cultures of our own.
You rise above all cultic claims
to answer to our many names,
a God as yet unknown.

O Wisdom, wait within us,
wake our weary hearts to praise,
empowering the powerless
and strengthening with gentleness,
till all embrace Your ways.

Our many paths all lead to You
in every time and place.
Our hearts rejoice in serving You,
make all we are and all we do
a channel of Your grace.

We turn to You, O Sacred Source
of hope and harmony.
Our work on earth will not be done,
till human hearts all beat as one
in global unity.

Loving You

The seed cups on my window sill offer a fast food service to a variety of resident and migrating birds as the years cycle through their seasons. Because my narrow desk is right up against the window, I have a ringside view of those wild, winged wonders whose flight path is a visible link between the heavens and rock-solid earth. Each time a feathered friend tarries to take and eat, it is I who am fed.

One day in the summer of 1995, I looked up from my book and found myself nose to nose with a chipmunk. The window was open and there was only a thin wire screen between us. Two little paws were firmly planted on the rim of a seed container, and two furry cheeks were already swollen with stolen contraband. As we stared at each other, I thought I caught a fleeting glimpse of eternity in those big, brown eyes, and it seemed like an eternity before one of us finally blinked. The first move was not mine. With the confidence of one long accustomed to having the final say, the chipmunk simply proceeded to finish its interrupted meal. That moment sealed our relationship, for this creature of the wild, whom I called "Stripes," had wiggled its way into my heart.

I should have seen it coming, had the sense to know it would not last. Then I could have invested some time in preparing for the end. I had first seen "my" chipmunk in early spring and I watched it grow from a wee one to twice its tiny size. It would run from the woods with lightning speed, dashing and darting to and fro, and then settle down, as still as a monk, to contemplate the world in solitude from the stone wall beneath my window. For an hour or so every morning, mute and motionless, it would look to the woods and savor life in a manner beyond my reckoning. Fellow mystic, I would sometimes say, we're on pilgrimage together. Do you see what I see? Know more than I can know?

For weeks we played at hide and seek. When I opened the window to replenish the seeds, my chipmunk scrambled for cover, watching with wide-eyed curiosity from a crevice between the stones. When I retreated, it swiftly devoured the spoils that had spilled to the ground from my fingers. As time went on, I began to place a mid-morning snack of sunflower seed and crushed corn on the stone wall for my companion. The new ritual, once established, seemed to deepen our bond. But enough was never enough. My chipmunk, who looked like a mouse with mumps, was food source for a family. Provisions had to be made against those blizzard-blown days to come, hard work when your only means of transport are pouches in your cheeks. Summer was swiftly slipping by. The cups on the ledge must surely have been a temptation beyond all telling. With a leap of faith one could land in the lap of luxurious supply.

"Stripes, however did you manage to get all the way up here?" I asked, when our eyes met that magical moment, but Stripes just licked the container clean, then went on to empty another until its cheeks bulged like balloons. The one who was usually scurrying about seemed in no hurry to be moving on, seemed to enjoy my company, was definitely pleased with the outcome of its daring initiative. As I watched my little stuffed animal friend leap onto a willowy, overgrown weed and somersault to the ground, I knew that with a will there was always a way and willed myself to seek a way to rise above the stress that accompanies a multi-

faceted life. Stripes returned again and again to the source that
offered sustenance, and all throughout that summer, from time
to time turned inward. From time to time, so did I.

A cold spell in early fall came unexpectedly. A fire was lit in
our fireplace, and more than twigs and timber went up in flames
that day. Looking back, I can say that the events that followed
rearranged the landscape of my spiritual life. I know the facts
only secondhand, for I was away that weekend, but this is what
I heard the moment I returned.

As soon as the fire was kindled and the smoke began to rise,
there was a rustling sound in the chimney, Mary Elizabeth said.
Then something fell into the ashes outside the circle of flames
and got up and took off in a flash. She said she did not know
what it was. It ran through the open door leading into the closed-
in porch, the room I call my sacred place, where I watch my
birds, talk to my chipmunk, and record my memories. She said
she thought it was a squirrel, but my heart said it was Stripes,
and no amount of descriptive data could convince me otherwise.
I was assured that whoever, whatever it was had returned to the
great outdoors, for the doors of the room had been shut and the
windows left wide open and it had not been seen again. The next
day I waited, and the day after that, but Stripes never came to
my window, nor did I see my mystical 'munk in the woods or on
the log or on the wall. I had a premonition of something, I know
not what, and it left me exceedingly sad.

On the third day I arose before dawn to walk, as I do most
days of the year. It was dark and I was barely awake as I sat at the
top of our basement steps to put on my walking shoes. When I
slipped my foot into my rundown Reebok, my toes touched something soft and silky tucked into the tip. Now why would I stuff
a stocking in there? That was the thought that came to mind,
for it felt like a bunched up nylon. I reached in and pulled it
out, and there in my hand was a furry little thing. For one split
second I froze. Then I leaped to my feet and let out a scream

that could have awakened Hartford. I opened my hand and drew
back in horror as the little fur ball flew through the air and fell
on the floor at my feet. I knew I had to look closer. I knew I
had to know, although the thought repelled me. I bent to exam-
ine the lifeless form and there they were, the stripes. And then I
began to cry. I cried like I hadn't cried in years as I walked full
speed through the neighborhood and all around the park. I cried
for Stripes. I cried for me. I cried for all the wounded and dead,
for all the victims of war and abuse and insensitivity. At least
that was what I was telling myself. Otherwise, how could I justify falling to pieces over a chipmunk when the whole world was
coming apart at the seams? I have always felt deeply the wounds
of the world. Now all that pent-up agony was finding its release.

There was no one around when I returned. Good, I thought,
for some experiences just have to be handled alone. I owed
Stripes a proper burial, but I knew absolutely nothing of the life-
cycle mores of chipmunks. I would put Stripes in the woods, I
decided, by the path that led to my window, where family members would discover the reason why their faithful provider was
never coming home. I arranged fall leaves around the remains —
gold and red and yellow — and tried to bury the guilt I felt at
having betrayed a trust. Stripes had felt safe and secure with me,
but that had led to disaster. No amount of rationalization could
fully erase my grief.

I called my Native American friend before the onset of winter
to probe for some deeper insight into all that had come to pass.
Pika confirmed what I already knew, that Stripes, trapped in a
three-story house, confused and terrified, had found a place of
refuge by curling up in my shoe. Secure in the scent of someone the chipmunk knew and loved and trusted, it chose the
moment and the place where its spirit joined with Great Spirit
for its final journey home. She also shared this interpretation for
my soul's benefit. The chipmunk had come as a spirit guide to
accompany me on a journey, as signified by my walking shoe. In-

deed, I was about to leave for India and a trip around the world. What on earth lay ahead, I wondered, that the Spirit would send this messenger to prepare the way for me? And what exactly was the message? Months would pass before the answers to those questions would be revealed.

After six exhausting, exhilarating months crisscrossing several continents and oceans and literally circling the globe, I was back at home in Hartford, ready to settle down for a while. I had been on more planes, trains, buses than I could name or number, had worn my sandals to shreds walking, had shed a number of pounds. It was a good feeling to be physically tired, yet emotionally and spiritually uplifted. There were no more trips in my schedule, and for once, I was honestly glad. Little did I know that the journey of a lifetime was just about to begin. It was one for which I was woefully unprepared, a venture unplanned and unexpected. I was about to enter unknown territory, barreling ahead without a map, and, for yet another time in my life, carrying too much baggage.

In mid-August a routine mammogram revealed multiple calcifications of a suspicious nature in my right breast. I was alone when I read the radiologist's report. On a malignancy scale of 1 to 5, with 5 representing highest probability, that which was growing inside of me had a 4–5 certainty of cancer. The horror implicit in that small word leaped out and enveloped me. Within the next few hours, I mentally rearranged everything short of planning my funeral liturgy, so certain was I that this report marked the end of the world for me. No matter what, it certainly was the end of the world as I had known it. I experienced an incredible sense of loss and a deep, penetrating sadness. Life would go on without me. All that was in flux would unfold and flourish and I would never know it. I felt keenly, existentially, my place in the universe. Infinitesimal. Transitory. Fragile. And ultimately, beyond my control. Yet I was glad that I had lived and for all that had been, I was grateful, overwhelmingly grateful. Then

I prayed, oh, how I prayed, for the willingness and the capacity
to accept all that was yet to be.

Time and a bit of common sense did much to restore a bal-
ance. I set out determined to be fully informed. I insisted on
receiving all written reports, asked endless questions, read *Dr. Su-
san Love's Breast Book*, an indispensable resource, attended her
Hartford lecture, and listened to breast cancer survivors who
offered their advice. I was determined that this need not be a
woman's best kept secret and spoke openly of my plight. I let
people minister to me and embraced prayer like a lifeline. A
biopsy confirmed multifocal ductal cancer. The good news: early
detection. The cancer was microscopic, although extremely ag-
gressive, and even though they did not get it all in the initial
surgery, what I had was noninvasive, meaning that it was con-
fined to the breast. I withdrew to review my options, put absolute
trust in my medical team of caring and competent physicians,
and prayed for grace and guidance.

I don't remember exactly when, but soon after reading my
mammogram results, when all was uncertain and I was distressed,
I received the first of several signs that God was journeying with
me, every step of the way. There on the stone wall outside my
window, gazing into the woods like a monk in contemplation,
I saw a tiny chipmunk, a miniature of Stripes. Suddenly in mid-
August, seemingly out of nowhere, as if it had come from another
dimension, I saw my spirit guide. Had it come to accompany me?
I felt comforted, as though I were actually gazing on an angel
in disguise. I also felt forgiven, and once again at peace with
the spirit of my woodland friend. The new chipmunk seemed to
know the routine. It looked for its seeds on the same stones fre-
quented by its parent, listened to my singsong chatter, helped
ground my reflections on life and death in the rhythms of the
universe, which is exactly where they belong.

More surgery lay ahead of me. After all the facts were in and
had been evaluated, I made my final decision on the strength

of my intuition. "What if" what is seen is not all that there is: that was the driving question, for I had dealt most of my life with things that are unseen. While mastectomy is never an easy choice and is now far more infrequent, it still remains an option, and that was the course I chose. Those whose opinions mattered most strongly supported my choice.

The surgery was scheduled for Thursday at dawn. On Monday I attended weekly chapel at Hartford Seminary and cried my way through the hymns. Afterward, Judy, my colleague and friend, who had lost her mother to breast cancer when she was in her teens, listened to this complaint. "Wouldn't you know," I said to her, "it took most of my life to discover a female image of God that's been truly nurturing. Shaddai, the Breasted One. Now it won't work for me anymore. The power has been drained out of it." And I mourned the loss of a connectedness that this name had given me. We cried. We hugged. We laughed. We left. Two hours later, I picked up my mail, and there was a box for me.

The return address said "Sacred Spaces." I knew it referred to a collection of feminist sculptures by a female artist friend, yet thought it serendipitous, given the way I felt. I opened the box and read the note. Betty was thanking me for inspiring her latest work, a sculpture of "Shaddai." She had been guided by what I had taught her in a lecture she had heard. I took out the piece of pottery, her depiction of Shaddai, and there was a God with wings.

Indeed, I teach Shaddai as both the breasted one and the winged one, showing how these images are both biblically based. In my pain, I had forgotten that, but in that transforming moment, I knew in the depth of my being that God Shaddai had reached out to me. In the moment of my deepest sorrow, when I felt like I was losing not only a part of myself but a dimension of the divine, God came to remind me that S/HE is with me, whatever the image or name. From that moment on, anxiety ceased. I felt myself enfolded within the sheltering wings of Shaddai.

The day before my surgery I had an evening class that I did

not have the heart to cancel. A number of students were partici-
pating. Its focus was spirituality. I needed to dwell on that. I don't
recall what I taught that night, but what I learned I will always
remember. At the end of class, my students encircled me and
sang a blessing over me. Something special happened that would
help me get through the next few days and through the rest of
my life. Two women could not wait to tell me how they had seen
my aura during the last hour of class, and how that aura, which
was bright yellow, grew larger and larger, spilling over onto others
during the blessing song. These women had not sat together, and
to them, seeing auras was a new experience. Yellow. The color
of God's indwelling presence. That is what I've been told. Again,
God gave a sign to me. The peace that I felt within me then was
all-encompassing, and it would never leave me during all that lay
ahead. God was with and within me. What did I have to fear?

The surgery went swiftly and smoothly. I sailed through it on
a stream of light. Both before and after, I felt borne along on a
wave of prayers, the prayers so many had promised and I could
feel were being said. Subsequent analysis proved my decision had
been the right one, for the breast had far more cancer, albeit
microscopic, than mammography had revealed. The chipmunk
remained outside my window through the first week of my recovery, and then it disappeared. Did it go into hibernation? Or did
it return to another realm? Only time will tell.

Loving You is wind on water, turbulence and storm,
loneliness laced with laughter, winter into warm.
Loving You is sometimes sunshine, even when it's raining.
Loving You means moving on, part of me remaining.
I'll see You in a million faces before my journey's through,
follow You to a million places, for a trace of You.
You're testing me at every turning where I taste Your love anew.
There's nothing lost, it's just the cost of loving You.
Nothing lost, it's the cost of loving You.

Loving You means no returning, always letting go,
starting over, ever learning, how well I know.
The One I love is all around me in all the love I'm feeling.
God above, let this love be Your own love's revealing.
I hear You reaching out to me in every anguished cry,
tempting me to stop awhile and watch the seasons by.
As I go, I'll go on living, even as I die.
There's nothing lost, it's just the cost of loving You.
Nothing lost, it's the cost of loving You.
Nothing lost, just the cost of loving . . . You.

Mother and God

Six months after my surgery I got a call from my mother, who lives in northern New Jersey. She was very upset. "I've got a lump in my breast," she said. "I'm going to the doctor. I can't let it go any longer." What she had was more than a lump in her breast. A large mass had broken through her skin and was suppurating and painful. Three days later they were preparing her for surgery. I went to be with her.

Why didn't you tell me? She answered my question before it left my lips. "I was going to tell you," she said, "but you had your own worries, and then it was Thanksgiving, and then it was Christmas. I thought I would wait until after the new year, but here it is, after Easter, and I can't wait any longer." We had sat around her kitchen table several times in the preceding months. I was there for the holidays she mentioned. I was there talking about my cancer, sharing each step of my journey from diagnosis to recovery. I thought it would make it easier to get such things out in the open when it came her time to do so. Obviously, I was wrong.

There may be a sea change in our willingness to talk openly about such terrifying topics as breast cancer and mastectomies, but the consequences of past decades of silence still come back to haunt us. Fear and an unwarranted sense of shame prevented the generations of our mothers and our grandmothers, our aunts and older sisters from speaking the unspeakable. Denial also played a role. Pretend it isn't there, and then it won't be real.

The ramifications are tragic. Without the comfort and support of others, fear turns into terror, reason enough not to attempt to make this journey alone. Without the opportunity to ask questions about new advances in medication and technology, without a clear picture of changing attitudes toward procedures, one is forever locked into outmoded methods, outdated data, and inaccurate statistics regarding life and death. As a result, the fears increase. In the absence of early detection and immediate medical attention, there is an escalation of both the disease and the risks.

Analysis is beside the point when you get to the point where we were. My mom was in a serious situation, and I could do nothing to help her. As they wheeled her through the double doors leading to the operating theater, I could see in her eyes the conviction that she would not come through them again. She looked so small on the gurney, so vulnerable and fragile, and young for her eighty-four-plus years. I would have traded places with her in a heartbeat, but that was not an option. So I did the one thing I knew I could do, pray up a storm and send to her those waves of healing energy that had so recently accompanied me and accomplished miracles within me.

Images of our life together — how brief the time we had together — washed over me as I waited. She is a warm and welcoming woman, kind and compassionate, self-sacrificing and self-effacing, one I would always turn to, the one I enjoyed just being with. I was the third child, her first girl, the child she chose to breast feed, a bond we share that has kept us close. "Take some money from my purse," she would say, when I was still a child. "Buy yourself an ice cream." We had so little when I was growing up in the flat above my grandfather's saloon, yet I was content with whatever we had. It may have been because I was not as assertive as my brothers that she would say to me now and then, "You should get something for yourself." I remember my first prom gown that we shopped for together, one that cost more than we could afford but was so beautiful, of white tulle and red velvet with a wide skirt lined with crinoline, when for one fleeting moment we were fairy godmother and Cinderella. She loved the energy I brought into the house, cheerleading, friends, hobbies, music, the dates, the dancing, the full extent of my love for life in the fifties. She took the news of my leaving home to enter a religious order far better than I had anticipated. "If that's what you want to do," she said. She was brave when face to face with me but cried a lot at night. That's what my father had told me.

I went for a formal interview a few months before graduation, when I was still sixteen. My mother accompanied me and came into the room with me, determined to see for herself what her daughter was getting into. Sister Pauline, in charge of vocations, tried to talk me out of it, suggesting I wait awhile because I was so young. I will never forget my mother's response. She had been silent until that moment. "What do you mean, she's too young? She's very mature. She knows what she wants. What do you mean, she shouldn't come?" Then she stopped, abruptly, wide-eyed, and said, "What am I doing? I came to talk her out of it, and here I am, talking you into it!" Nevertheless, she held her ground. Talk them into it she did, talked them into taking me, because that was what I wanted, what I felt called to be and do. I went home periodically through the years, but only for a visit, not an extended stay. My letters from around the world shared highlights of my adventuresome life and my mom read them avidly. Our lives developed differently and apart from one another. We were never again caught up in the daily together until now. After forty-some years, here I was, walking the halls of a hospital, awaiting word of the woman who had been a widow for twenty-three of those years, a woman named Irene, who was, who is my mother.

She came through surgery successfully and made a quick re-covery, relieved just to be alive. When I brought her back to her own home, we had one set of breasts between us, and for us that would be enough. On one level she was fine; on another there was the silence, the denial, and, underneath that, the fear. I returned to Connecticut but went back again when her anxiety increased, went with her for her checkups, tried to help her give voice to the fear that was manifesting itself now in various pains in other parts of her body. At least I hoped it was the fear and not another form of cancer.

Several weeks after her surgery I was preparing for a bene-fit concert to raise funds for needy children, an annual event for Connecticut's kids that I do with my friend Don. This year's theme was "Ark Angels," and Frankie, an artist in my community, had built an enormous ark for me out of corrugated cardboard, a vessel Noah would have envied. We filled the ark with stuffed animals of every size and shape and a multitude of species and also with Cabbage Patch dolls who seemed eager to sign on for the ride. The ark sailed over the waves beneath a dazzling rain-bow. My Medical Mission Sisters choir joined us for song and liturgical dance to make it an evening to remember. After it was over we stayed up nearly half the night relishing its sound and spirit.

The next day my sisters took to the road, and after the ark had been dismantled, the animals and dolls dispersed to wher-ever they had come from, I decided to rest for a little while. It was already noon, the week had been exhausting, and I had run out of steam. My head had barely touched the pillow when the telephone rang. It was my brother Jack, who shares the house with my mother. "Come, quick," he said in a panic. "Mom is in the hospital." He went on to explain that when she didn't get up at her usual hour he went to her room to wake her, that he found her barely able to speak, that her bottle of pain pills was empty, that the ambulance came and took her to the emergency room, they had treated her and were holding her there until someone made a decision. He said he didn't know what to do and to hurry up and get there. I began to move with an energy I didn't know I had in me, threw some things in the trunk of the car, swiftly cleared my calendar, and spent three agonizing hours heading south with Mary Elizabeth into I knew not what. From the pinnacle of an emotional high of ark angels and Spirit and song and a pot of gold for children at risk at the end of a colorful rainbow, I plummeted into the depths of a pain so sharp and penetrating its scar will remain forever.

Seeing my mom in that windowless cubicle, as she cried out in anguish and pain and a guilt that knew no mercy, is all I'll ever need to know of hell. If one doubts the power of images or the strength of their tenacity, go ahead and try to eliminate such a scene from the archive of the mind. I felt overwhelming compassion for her, tried to be the strength she no longer had, the hope she had lost in the darkness, the tangible proof that there was such a thing as unconditional love and that God and I both had it, had such a love for her. I just wanted it to end, she said, the pain, the fear, the worry. How could I have done such a thing? I'm sorry. I'm so sorry. I just meant to take one pill for the pain. Then somehow I took another. And another. It's okay, Mom, I tried to assure her. I'm here and I won't leave you, and my love for you is the same.

It is state law in such circumstances to admit to a psychiatric ward, which only increased her trauma. I don't belong here, she cried. She was right, but I could do nothing about it. She slept a lot in the days ahead. She had not fully recovered from her extensive surgery before her body had taken another hit, leaving her physically miserable, emotionally distraught, and spiritually destitute. When she was released it was into my care, and we took her with us to Hartford. My brother was so grateful that he later gave me a very touching gift, a most prized possession that ranked second only to his Thunderbird car. He gave me his

Martin guitar. He had thought he would have to go it alone, that since I was in the convent, he could no longer count on me. Thanks be to God he was wrong.

My mom had never been to Hartford, had never seen the big old seminary house where we lived. She rarely traveled. She didn't drive. To leave her home to come so far was yet another thing she had to suffer and endure. For the first few days all she did was sleep and eat and sleep some more. By the end of the week she began to take notice of her surroundings. She smiled one morning, and then she laughed, and then slowly returned to normal. The rest of this narrative is a witness to the power of prayer and the gift of love and a lifetime of fidelity that brings its own reward, for it was this woman herself, with all her goodness, grace, and humor, that turned her life around.

Our simple rituals focused on food. Her sheer delight in whatever I served, the fact that someone served her at all, that I, her daughter, was cooking for her, was for me a blessing. I had left home at seventeen without a clue about boiling an egg and now was able to demonstrate the benefits of years of preparing meals daily outside the enclosure walls. Whenever I eat oatmeal, Mom, or cream of wheat or buttered bread or rice or cabbage noodles, I will remember you. If ever a meal were a eucharist, these meals that brought you back to life and our lives to the fullness of meaning, these simple meals at home with you were eucharist for me. We came to know each other again, grew closer than I could ever have hoped in the years that were remaining. We laughed, told stories, went for walks, and exchanged recipes. She began to speak of all those things she could not mention before. We talked at length about cancer and the ways in which I would be part of her life in the time that she had remaining. We spoke of her attempted suicide, not right away but when it was time, and acknowledged those things that had driven her to give up on life, to give up on herself, and to turn her face from God. She knew that God had forgiven her when she finally was able to forgive herself. A turning point was my conviction, my unwavering conviction, that her desperate act was a gift, not a curse, because it brought us together again in ways we would never have known, gave us the opportunity to address the fears that enslave us, gave us a chance to remind ourselves that God is a God of love and not judgmental retribution. I believed then, as I do now, that I was the one in dire need of a monumental wake-up call to reorder my priorities. The suffering brought us blessings that we knew were worth the cost. Once again crucifixion gave rise to unprecedented benefits of relationship and shalom. God was in all of this somewhere. I've seen the telltale fingerprints on the surface of my heart.

When she was back in her own home again, she returned to Mass at her parish church. She took all the Sunday offering envelopes that had been accumulating for months and put money in every one. Six weeks later she called to say the tumor was growing back. I praised her for seeing it and saying so. She came to Hartford for surgery and a full course of radiation. She remembered everything and everyone that she had met the first time around. Her memory, her sense of humor, and her interest in people are her very special gifts. We had more time to do things together, like going door to door for trick-or-treat, which was the first time she had taken part in this Halloween ritual. Let me tell you she took that bag full of candy directly to her room and it was never seen again. Three months after she returned to her home, my younger sister, Marilyn, lost both of her breasts to cancer. Now there are three of us in this together with one set of breasts among us.

I've written extensively of this, not only to tell my mother's story, which is so much a part of my own story, but also to help break the silence surrounding yet another taboo. The issue of suicide or attempted suicide needs to be addressed forthrightly in the church, with understanding and compassion. So does the relationship between such an act and God. All those condemnations, which were said to be God's condemnation, hung like barnacles from my mother's heart and very nearly destroyed her. That is not to say we should condone suicide, but neither should we categorically condemn it. As my mother was leaving the psychiatric ward with a deeply troubled psyche, her roommate sidled up to me and with eyes as big as saucers said quietly, "I am doomed." She told me she was Catholic, that she had attempted to take her life, that she could never be forgiven, and that God would never forgive her. The church had told her so. No one had been to visit her, not that I could see. She seemed intrigued by my concern for my mother and by the fact that I had accepted whatever had occurred. I sensed that she too was hungering for a forgiving word. Torn between her need and my mother's departure — she was already on her way out the door — I could only say, "God loves you. Don't ever doubt God's love for you. God loves you and forgives you." The image of her sad face haunts me still and I sense that, in the burden she carries, she is not alone.

Another theme we need to revisit is the issue of life after death, or life after life, or simply afterlife, which is life's continuity. I know this really troubled my mom, and she questioned me once about that. Is there really a life after this one? Is there really a heaven like they told us about? If there is, then where did everyone go? Surely, with all that travel in space, they should have met someone by now. I wanted to hug her. She is so real. All those theological nuances of the body remaining buried until the final judgment at the end of time when all will rise again together had sailed right over her head. I'm sure the same is true for many.

The theory of quantum physics that suggests that the cosmos may live forever puts the final judgment in jeopardy. Quantum theology has addressed this issue. Sadly, the church has not, which means a lot of Christian people have nowhere to turn and no one to talk to regarding this most significant question: what happens at the end of life? All I could say to my mother is what

I have said to myself. There is no definitive answer because it remains a mystery. This much I intuit: inherent to all of life is the life-force of the spirit, which is one with God's own Spirit, and this spirit never dies. In this spirit we live on. I cannot know what form it will take, but I know I will go on living and be part of all that lives and dies and rises to live again. The moment my mother chose to check out was the moment she felt there was nothing at the end but an end to her present suffering. Old theologies no longer seemed to make much sense to her, and since the church has not offered a vision to take us through these troubling times nor encouraged us to think on these things, my mother simply took the step toward which her logic had led her. I think she thinks differently now.

I would not have told this story without my mother's permission, and just to complete the circle, let me tell you how that came about. She returned to Hartford for a summer vacation while I was writing this book. I had just completed my reflections on the Spirit when I felt the Spirit give me a song — a melody, a phrase or two, and a sense of where it was heading. I did not want to interrupt the book to turn my attention to it, so I put it aside for in-between times, its structure secure in my heart. Throughout the day, I had been anguishing over my mother's story, how and if I should tell it, how and if I should ask if I could, and hesitating to do so. I went to bed early with the song on my mind, which would be a song of the Spirit.

I woke up in the dead of night. A breeze came through my windows. I heard the whir of wings. I thought I was imagining things, but there it was again. Definitely wings. A breeze? Wings? The Holy Spirit! The Spirit had come to give me the words to the song She would have me sing. The sound grew more insistent, now here, now there, circling the room. Suddenly, I was apprehensive. What if it's a bird, a really big bird, and not the Holy Spirit? What if there's a bird in my bedroom? I drew my sheet up over my head, reached for the switch and threw on the light, and when I had the courage to look, saw an enormous black wingspread wildly circling my room. Well, it looked enormous to me, although the hero of this story would eventually say it was a bat, not a bird, and nowhere near the size I had imagined. I slid onto the flood, crawled out of the room, and shut the door behind me with a bang and an exclamation. "Are you all right?" my mother asked. Her room is adjacent and she's often awake. "No, I'm not!" And I told her. Discussion. Laughter. It has to be a bat, she said from experience, and went on to tell a lengthy and funny bat story of her own.

Mary Elizabeth came down from her third-floor room, awakened by the ruckus, and went in and opened the windows, retrieved my clothes and my walking shoes and anything I might need in the morning, and that was that until we met at breakfast and the story picked up again. Since I had to write this piece that morning, I asked my mom how she would feel if I wrote about her cancer. "Is there anything you want me to leave out?" I asked. "Write whatever you want," she said, and that was the end of it. A burden lifted from my heart and rose on an eagle's wings. "The Spirit is no nesting dove." Hadn't I written of that before? "Where the Spirit is, there is chaos," a chaos preceding creativity. In the time between 3:00 a.m. and breakfast, following the chaos of whirring wings in the darkest part of the night, verses of the song had come to me, were given to me by the Spirit. "You are the melody, I am the word of our song. Sing to Me, sing of Me, and I will be singing along." The bat was a means of connecting with my mom on a story-telling level, paving the way for me to pursue permission to tell her story so that others in similar circumstances might know that there is hope and possibility for transformation. Yes, that was the Spirit, I said to myself, and laughed at the incongruity and absurdity and serendipity of it all. Such is the way of the Spirit. Of this I am absolutely certain.

As I complete this reflection on my mother, I am reminded of a time in Botswana on the rim of the Kalahari in southern

Africa where I gave a course to indigenous women. One day
we were sharing about life after life and they spoke about their
ancestors, who are as real to the African as a living person is
real to you and me. The women of Zimbabwe and Zambia said
that whenever they wanted something, they would go to their
mother who would go to her mother, who went to her mother,
who went to her mother... to her mother... to her mother... to
her mother... all the way back to the beginning of time to the
mother who went to the mother of God who went directly to
God. The answer came back the same way, from God back to
the present, giving a sense of daughter and mother, mother and
daughter, in a long, grace-full, unbroken line all the way back
and directly into the heart of our mothering God. I have felt
this mother-daughter connection with my own mother and our
Mother God, and this has been for me the clearest of signs of the
Spirit in our lives.

> Mother and God, to You we sing:
> wide is Your womb, warm is Your wing.
> In You we live, move, and are fed,
> sweet, flowing milk, life-giving bread.
> Mother and God, to You we bring
> all broken hearts, all broken wings.

Mystery

I like to walk the day awake as fresh morning air wipes sleep from my eyes and the birds sing all around me.

Good morning, God.
Good morning, morning.
Thank You for this day.
Thank You for life, for the love of living,
for Your spirit's empowering ways.
I praise You and give glory to You
through all Your images and names.
Thank you for yesterday,
for the good Your love accomplished
in my life and in our universe.
Forgive my faults and failings.
Forgive my participation
in the sin of global injustice
and systemic inequities.
Speak to me and through me the word
You would have me speak to others,
and help me receive and believe the word
You speak through others to me.

I offer You all that I do and am
for Your mission and Your ministries
in service of Your people
and for the healing of Your planet.
Holy Your compassionate Presence.
Holy Your manifest images.
Holy Your manifold names.
Awaken Your spirit within me,
that I might see Your path for me
and be substantially changed.
Our Mother, our Father,
on earth and in heaven,
give us today sufficient bread
to make it through tomorrow,
and fill everyone everywhere
with the fullness of shalom.
As I enter into communion this day
with all Your children, all creation,
let me nourish and be nourished,
nurture and be nurtured,
bless and be a blessing,
and help me to know and understand
that everything that comes my way
is You blessing me.

Down sidewalks wearing invisible signs of all who have walked
before me, I weave in and out of streetlight and shadow into the
first bright blush of dawn in a ritual celebration of the liturgy
of life.

My two-mile walk past Sunrise Overlook into and through an
inner-city park mirrors a young girl's earlier walks down other
roads in other times with a much smaller world within her. It
is spirit time, centering time, a time of intuitive insights, of letting imagination take me wherever it would have me go, a time

when sometimes songs and poems awaken and take wing, a time for communing with One who, for want of a better all-purpose designation, we simply call "God."

> Wisdom moves among us when day is done.
> Hers the spark that lights the dark and births the rising sun.
> Wisdom, deep within us, directs our days.
> Marvelous Her love of us, mysterious Her ways.
>> Come to Me. Lean on Me, your Rock and Rod.
>> Come to Me. Taste and see how good, how very good, is God.

Recovering from my encounter with cancer I found, as always, that walking helped me integrate this new relational dimension into my catalogue of experience and my emerging sense of self. Song translated experience into metaphor and meaning on yet another plane.

> Wisdom's healing waters, the tears we've cried,
> come and go, their ebb and flow is Love's eternal tide.
> Wisdom weaves Her blessings with ties that bind.
> All who long shall hear Her song and all who seek shall find.
>> Come to Me. Lean on Me, your Rock and Rod.
>> Come to Me. Taste and see how good, how very good, is God.
> Wisdom wakes the spirit that never dies,
> making all who heed Her call compassionate and wise.
> Wisdom, always with us, designing ways
> to rehearse the universe in universal praise.

Whoever has walked with wisdom through the darkness into the day, loving both shade and shadow as passionately as the light, can only be mystified when anyone stops to question the legitimacy of Wisdom (Sophia) as an image and name for God.

In the best of times, which is summertime when the schedule is much less stressful, there is time for further reflection before the continuation of the day.

Sit. Relax. Take three deep breaths,
big belly breaths, lung filling breaths.
Let all the tension throughout your body
slough off and fall away.
Three more breaths, deep, filling.
Breathe in Spirit,
letting Spirit fill every crevice of your body,
every aspect of your being,
every dimension of soul and spirit.
Breathe in Light,
pulling it down and in from above
through the top of your head to the tips of your toes,
to your fingertips and vital organs,
letting Light seep into you to enlighten you within.
Breathe in Energy,
pulling it up and in from below,
from the bedrock of earth, from soil and stone
and all earth's life-giving waters,
from the roots of trees and their leaves and branches,
letting earth's Energy permeate you
to energize bone and marrow
and pulse through every single cell as spirit energy.
Deep within your center,
breathe in recognition of,
exhale intermingling of
vital empowering power
of Spirit, Light, Energy
as Life, Wisdom, Love —
Spirit of Life
Light of Wisdom
Energy of Love —
Living Spirit
Enlightening Wisdom
Energizing Love —

> a life force
> a faith force
> residing within
> and reaching out
> to accompany you into the world.

In the best of times there is enough time to begin the day with a focus on that which really matters, even if only for a moment or two or only now and then. After that, the daily challenge: to discern within the whirlwind the still small voice of Spirit and respond accordingly. Before falling asleep, I like to say a rosary, a rediscovery and revitalization of what was my daily prayer for years before the winds of renewal and change blew my beads away. I have added to the traditional Mysteries that accompany this prayer — mysteries of Spirit, healing, jubilee, mysteries of life and love and longing — and pray these like a mantra for all those who have asked my prayers, for all those for whom I promised to pray, for all the needs and wounds of the world for which I feel the need to pray. It reconnects me to my roots and brings a note of serenity and closure to my day.

I speak a lot about imaging God, about re-imaging or re-imagining, because images are important. God-images are important. They influence our behavior, shape our self-understanding, determine our religious response and our relationship to others, mediate what we know about God or what we think we know. Images are those aspects of God that touch our life concretely for better or for worse, evoking enthusiasm or apathy, intimacy or detachment, giving rise to hope or despair or simply indifference.

A long time ago, when I was young, I was taught to image God as Father. That image nourished me through the years and still has the capacity to work for me now and then. As time went on, I added other images directly from tradition, images of power and might, of judgment and domination, of tenderness and steadfast love. Those biblical images, liturgical images, images of religious piety were, for the most part, patriarchal and male, which may have been why I preferred images that arose from the natural world. Water, rock, whirlwind, storm, rising sun, morning star, burning bush, tree of life, One who rides on the wings of the wind and thunders across the waters: such images are foundational to my vocabulary of faith. Other images from the Bible, like "still small voice" and "new song," also became integral to my prayer. Such images touched me deeply and became a part of me, perhaps because they were clearly metaphors, spoken as if I had said them myself, for our language was the same. It took a very long time before I came to realize that all God-images are metaphors, every one, without exception. They arose from the human endeavor to connect with the divine, either from an individual's heartfelt cry or a community's articulation, a spontaneous or considered outpouring of passion or praise that reflected an experience of love, deliverance, trust, faith, anger, regret, or desperation at some time in history. That realization was a turning point in my understanding of how relative is all our conversation, read theology here, about God.

Indeed, God is Absolute, the only Absolute, and we who are finite creatures from whatever culture, time, or place, whatever gender, race, age, condition, or social situation can only know God relatively, which means metaphorically, which means not literally, which means what we know can change. I lived into my understanding of God as maternal, as Mother, through my experience as a woman in touch with many other women. God as pregnant woman, midwife, nursing mother, courageously protective of her endangered offspring, tender and nurturing, would never forget or abandon the child She had conceived and carried and brought to birth, the child who once was as helpless and as trusting as a nursing baby, and at times still is. It was through a female perspective conditioned and expanded by the diversity and the experience of women around the world that I discovered the depth of the feminine dimension and the many female aspects of the God of my tradition. My abiding love for the biblical word in spite of all of its limitations and patriarchal irrelevancies led me to uncover those ancient roots underlying emerging images celebrating She Who Is and to know that these are as much a part of tradition as images that are male.

It took less time to realize that we who are created in the image of God, as Genesis insists, have re-created God in the image of ourselves, in the image of only a few of us, and promulgated those few metaphors as unassailable facts, as all-inclusive truth. We who are created in the image of God were created female and male according to Genesis, indicating women do image God in the understanding of tradition, which means that all humanity images — mirrors — God (Gen. 1:27). Look into any human face and see the face of God.

Because women reflect an image of God, it is theologically justifiable to image God as female. Biblical tradition has. Once we are open to this, it is amazing how often we find it reflected in canonical texts. I especially enjoyed discovering Shaddai as an ancient image and name for God. In Jacob's blessing of Joseph, his beloved Rachel's beloved son, he asks that God "Shaddai" bless him with "blessings of the breasts and of the womb" (Gen. 49:25). Shaddai, a designation that occurs approximately forty-eight times in the Hebrew Scriptures, arises from the Hebrew word for breast (*shad*) — God "the breasted one." Also, God "the winged one," to whom the psalmist turned in times of danger and distress, praying: we who shelter in the shadow of Shaddai trust that She will cover us with her pinions, that we will find refuge under Her wings (Ps. 91:1–4). It is the image Jesus invoked in Jerusalem, with which he identified when he lamented: "How often have I desired to gather your children together as a hen gathers her brood under her wings" (Matt. 23:37). Shekinah, sacred presence, abiding indwelling presence, and Wisdom (Sophia) who was with God from the beginning and is God, are God-images and names we glean from sacred Scripture. These have nourished me through the years, as has the image of Shalom. *Naamoni aiyai,* the Masaii women of Kenya in East Africa sing: "The She to whom I pray." *Onyame Bataan Pa,* Ghanaian women of West Africa pray: "Good Mother God...nursing mother God." Now we too pray the same.

Images are not essential. I knew God long before I imaged God and there have always been gaps of time, including now in this present time, when the experience and the relationship transcend all images. Sometimes, however, we need images, or simply delight in them. Our images give access to the Inaccessible One, bringing the seemingly distant closer to facilitate our perceiving, building ladders that help us cross between that other realm and ours. They make the Invisible visible, tangibly link the Eternal Now to our fleeting, finite present, are a means of communication and an expression of intimacy. When we need them, we should use them, and when we feel they are unnecessary, we should simply let them go.

There is a close relationship between our images and our names for the God of our many traditions. Images arise when we set out to name the God of our experience. To name is to draw God close in ways that are distinct, concrete, and intensely personal. Spiritually, as in everyday life, we may name someone we have come to know in a way that seals our relationship and has impact on our lives. All well and good with respect to God, as long as we avoid inordinate claims, saying we know more than we know, claiming to know the God we have named in ways beyond our naming. God is a God of infinite names. We know but a finite number and accept even less than that, but the few we have and the little we know are at least a bit more than we knew before we had the names.

In one sense names are irrelevant, for they limit and exclude. On the other hand, names are like windows into facets of reality that might otherwise remain unknown. For instance, my birth name is Gloria. I relinquished it when I took the habit and became my other names. I have been Miriam Therese far longer than I have been Gloria, yet I am still Gloria, because that is my name. When other sisters went back to their birth names along with the postconciliar changes, I kept my name in religious life because it had become associated with the songs I pray and sing, not only to others, but especially to me. Names are associational, accumulating bits and bundles of meaning from a multitude of contexts, giving access to those persons who can relate to given experiences when they call upon our name. My mother told me not long ago that she said after giving birth to me: "Glory be to God, it's a girl!" That's why she gave me the name. Now I know why I felt so special singing the Latin *Gloria* at Mass and the *Gloria in excelsis Deo* in Christmas carols and chants. There are moments when we are our names. My name reminds me of who I am, an exclamation of thanks and praise to the all-knowing, all-loving God of my being, and the cause of my mother's joy. To my mom I will always be Gloria, and I respond to her that way. To most people I am Miriam Therese, to some I am simply Miriam, and to students and others I have known for years, I answer to M.T.

If I can have these different names that reveal different images and aspects of me, imagine how many images and names we might need, might have, should have for God in order to experience as many of the limitless facets of God's reality as is humanly possible. Even then, if we imagined all the God-images it were possible to imagine and named every name we could possibly name, we would still come nowhere near expressing the immensity, the incomprehensibility of God. Our images and names do nothing to God, they certainly do not change God, but they do a lot for us. They change our perceptions of God, allow us to grow or confine us to the stifling restrictions of metaphoric idolatry. Because every image limits and every name constructs a frame, more images extend the limits, more names enlarge the frame, so that the box we tend to put God in is at least big enough for more of God's creation to find room within it. My favorite names for God these days are Mystery, Spirit, Presence, Energy, perhaps because I can apply multiple images to each of these names or simply savor the explicit God-reality implicit within them. What is most important of all to me is what these images do to deepen my relationship with God and my relationship with God's creation, and with all that lives within it.

> It's the song of the universe, as the aeons fall away.
> It's the song that the stars sing and all the planets play.
> It's a song to the Power neither you nor I can see.
> It's a song to the One who is Mystery.

All of our images and names, both ancient and newly evolving, tend to entangle us in a net of theological expectations. To get caught in those traps is to miss the point, which is theophany: God's self-revelation in the universe of human experience in and through the limitations of our images and names.

The topic of revelatory images and names is particularly relevant to an understanding of Jesus. My childhood images of Jesus were formed by the pictures I had hung all over the walls of my bedroom when I was still a young girl. Good Shepherd. Sacred Heart. One who stands at the door and knocks. King of Kings. Lord of Lords. Metaphors all, I know that now, but I took them literally then. Metaphors change with the changing times and with personal and community perspective. One's story can be told so many ways — I tell my own story in different ways — to uncover its inherent wisdom, both for the teller and for those to whom it is told.

The Jesus story for me now has a whole new set of images that arise out of the same biblical texts. A lifetime of experience has enabled me finally to see them. I see Jesus as one who was homeless for a time. Like any street person with a makeshift shelter, he too slept in a borrowed bed, a feed trough for animals. Like any ordinary child he was nourished at his mother's breast, and she, as any mother would, must surely have gazed on her baby and said, "Bone of my bone, flesh of my flesh, yours is my body, yours is my blood." He spent his infancy on the run and ended up in exile. He acted like a typical teenager, scaring his parents half to death with his thoughtless disappearance when he stayed behind in Jerusalem, an adolescent know-it-all who enjoyed outwitting his teachers. As an adult he took to the open road, moving around from place to place with a somewhat dysfunctional group of men and some liberated women, sharing a vision with anyone who happened to listen to him. He fulfilled none of the criteria for a career path to success as defined by the times in which he lived. He had no children — he had no son — in fact he never married. He seemed to have no fixed address, and we always find him having a meal at somebody else's table. From what we know, he was unemployed and not particularly religious, except in his own way. He hung out with the ostracized, challenged unjust structures, riled authorities, shattered precedent, dismissed protocol, broke the rules, reinterpreted tradition, incited the masses to think for themselves, made what seemed to be extravagant claims, acted in ways that defied explanation, and cajoled people far and wide to reorder their priorities. If someone like this showed up at your door, would you let your daughter marry him?

Jesus was a man filled with the Spirit, one who acted in ways transformative for women and for men. He proclaimed a new understanding of God, a new description of God's people. He repudiated the religious and social elite for their arrogance, their insensitivity, and their patriarchal privilege, for which he was brutally executed, but his spirit, his power live on. This is the Jesus I know and love, whose incarnate wisdom I cherish, whose ways I would enflesh. His passion for justice, his compassionate presence have even more relevance and meaning now and are spiritual anchors for me. My images of Jesus have changed and they will continue to change, but his spirit within and beyond all images abides and remains the same.

Long after his physical image faded his death was reinterpreted as theological necessity, as though God had required it, allowing the evil that eliminated him to survive to eliminate us, allowing it to surreptitiously and insidiously influence us to use the very death of Jesus to abuse and eliminate others in memory of him. The massacre of so-called enemies, nonbelievers, and nonconformists, the holocaust and other genocides, planetary geocide, war, executions, suppression, oppression, enslavement, rape, cruelty, violence, discrimination, and abuse have all been linked to and justified by a God-image and its interpretations. The God who gives life was re-imaged as the God who takes life away. The Crusades, the Inquisition, interdenominational wars, witch hunts and hangings and burning at the stake, the destruction of indigenous peoples, the brutalization of those we enslaved, to name but a few, have added chapter after bloody chapter to the history of the church — all in the name of God or with God's tacit approval, or so we have been told. We worship a God whom we imagine demanded his own son's death as satisfactory retribution for a flawed humanity. Did God really want this? Or did we imagine it? Did we re-image God as an image of ourselves and thereby justify our destructive tendencies?

Death by fire or the sword is one thing, but no less violent have been the ways we kill one another more discreetly, with our words or with our laws, cutting people off from the Body of Christ through condemnation or excommunication. Ours is a faith tradition oriented more toward death and dying than calling forth and encouraging life. Deprivation has long been a Christian virtue. Merit is gained through sacrifice and discipleship through submission. Fidelity requires that we put to death all arising within and around us that is contrary to orthodoxy. Our silence before our accusers perpetuates the lengthy precedent that kills our desires and our dreams.

We Christians who are so adept at scourging the demons within us and nailing ourselves to the cross are also a little too inclined to do the same unto others. Kill the killers. Execute. A life for a life, death for a death. On the threshold of death Jesus cried out: "Forgive them, for they know not what they do." Dear God, forgive us. You know we know exactly what we do. We are perilously close to missing the point of why we call ourselves Christians. A deep river of violence seems to lie just below the surface of our patriarchal church. What happened to Jesus is a vivid reminder of what happens to those who would dare defy the dictates of domination. The death done unto Jesus is the death we do unto others and the death done unto us. There is a fine line distinguishing perpetrator from victim and a chasm separating mercy from our own self-righteousness. No matter how tightly we shut our eyes, we can still see the crucified Jesus impaled against the sky. When we look at the cloth that wiped his face, we see our own face upon it, yet we who believe in Jesus and in all that he envisioned still choose to follow him.

Once a year we rally around the resurrected One and behave like Easter people, while the rest of the time we are shaped by a rite with crucifixion at its core. Our hearts are attuned to an invitation to "remember the death of Jesus until he comes again." We celebrate the One who was broken, whose blood was savagely shed, and in the liturgical process often become what we justify. We are the body broken. Ours is the life force that seeps away as we fall beneath the heavy weight of religious expectations and hang there in the interim until Jesus comes again. One truth we have yet to assimilate is that to remember the death of Jesus means to remember the life that led up to the death and the life that rose to defy it. We are essentially Resurrection people. We embrace the One who came that we might have life in all its fullness, and we follow Jesus whose whole existence was oriented toward life. Jesus proclaimed the fullness of life, not just for us but for everyone, our competitors as well as our friends, life as expressed through the life of Jesus before and after death, life that is life-giving, life that will live on. Resurrection people are committed to bringing the dead to life. A very close friend once said to me, "You gave me back my life." The words touched me deeply. We give back life in so many ways, by listening to one who feels lost and alone, by being fully present to pain, by accepting and loving regardless, by giving life to those whom others keep telling to "get a life," by living our lives in life-giving ways.

When we finally recognize God-with-us already in our midst, we realize that Mary's child was a lot like the people we are trying to keep out of our neighborhoods, people previously incarcerated or of lower economic status, people we unfairly label as different from ourselves. "Remember, I am with you always" (Matt. 28:20). Encouraging words, Jesus, yet where on earth were you when we were called to account for our actions and our visions and our impossible dreams? I was right there all around you, we hear, in the poor, the hungry, the homeless, the sick, the incarcerated, the outcast, the victims of abuse and of racial and economic discrimination. The Christ we await and boldly proclaim is never quite what we are looking for, which is why the question of images is especially pertinent. It is time we resurrected the forces of life-giving life in ourselves and in our institutions. Through random acts of kindness and intentional works of mercy, through advocacy for justice on behalf of those oppressed, through challenges to systemic intolerance under guidance of the Spirit, and through an acceptance of those who seem beyond our understanding, we name and proclaim how the risen Christ is transforming our world and its people.

Every morning of every day an Easter Sun rises, making a mockery of our subconscious fears of an everlasting night. Embracing life in the face of death is the call we are to incarnate. Death has many disguises. Life has need of none. We may not always know what is killing us, but we know what gives us life. Something rises within us to remind us, if only for a moment, that it is good to be alive. Easter is the moment when we who are called to image Christ, women as well as men, know we are

Easter people because we feel our sluggish spirits suddenly ener-gized by Life. A fitting response to the Easter greeting "Christ is risen" would be: "We are risen indeed, alleluia!" Perhaps it is only through you and me and all committed people that Christ comes again. And again.

Remnants of an ancient time of communal peace and har-mony still inhabit our universe, surfacing from time to time like the sound of a long forgotten song, inspiring a vision of blessed-ness and the will to bring it about. These resonate throughout the Bible in variations of healing and wholeness, of justice and compassion, of gentleness and peace, coming to a climax in the person of Jesus. His compassion for those outside the circle bears witness to us of the spirit of God's all-encompassing love. That spirit lives among us wherever one or two or more embody the spirit of God's own Spirit of universal peace.

The spirit of God, the spirit of Jesus, the one we call Holy Spirit: we are speaking of one Spirit, one all-inclusive Spirit reflecting humanity's experience of core life-giving aspects of Di-vine Oneness, another image/name for God. It is the spirit of Divine Oneness who calls forth as Creating One, is embodied as Incarnate One, is empowering, inspiring, energizing as Indwelling One, in and through me, in and through you, in and through all faith-filled people. This is all I need to know of God. The rest is Mystery.

> When I stand on a rolling hill and I look out to the sea,
> I can feel the force of freedom finding fellowship with me.
> I can hear a call to courage to be all that I might be.
> Then I know I have known Mystery.
>
> When I walk through a wooded grove to admire nature's art,
> I can feel her weave her wisdom on the webbing of my heart.
> I can hear her invitation to be part of all I see.
> Then I know I have known Mystery.

As I run through the sunlight and the shadows of the years,
I can feel a strong sensation through the silence of the spheres.
I can hear a call to loving all, to immortality.
Then I know I have known Mystery.

It's the song of the universe, as the aeons fall away.
It's the song that the stars sing and all the planets play.
It's a song to the Power neither you nor I can see.
It's a song to the One who is Mystery.

You Come Bringing Music

The plane banked, the clouds broke, the golden light of late afternoon spilled out of the sky and rushed to embrace the rolling hills of Connecticut. Spirit sang: "God of my childhood and my call." My heart responded: "Make me a window, not a wall." Another song sang itself into life before the day was over.

God of my childhood and my call,
make me a window, not a wall.
So like an icon, may I be
a sign of love's transparency,
and through the love that lives in me,
proclaim Your lasting love for all.

Come, O my Maker, make of me
a mirror, so that all may see
within themselves Your saving grace,
reflection of Your Holy Face,
an image of Your warm embrace
and nurturing reality.

Creator, re-create us all.
Come, lift us up before we fall.
You are the Wisdom and the Way,
the Dawning of Unending Day,
the Word we sometimes fail to say
within our canon of recall.

God of our future, help us see
a vision of the yet-to-be:
in You is freedom from our fears,
a silent strength and no more tears;
in You dissention disappears
into a global harmony.

God of all gods, to You we sing
a song of Your imagining:
a liberating melody,
to set our shackled spirits free,
to tell us that Your canopy
of care is all-encompassing.

I have always sung about God. I am drawn instinctively to this awesome theme like a butterfly to a field of flowers. There is always more to discover about God, more to imagine and feel and express, so much more in the relationship to deepen and to know. Music has infinite potential for evoking God-images and names. The biblical psalms, which were originally sung, reflect this integral connection between music and theophany. Music also prepares the heart to be less literal and more imaginative, helping us see the poetic and prophetic potential in biblical prose.

Once when I felt the fire within and believed I was standing on holy ground, Spirit opened a window into a wellspring of meaning in a familiar biblical text. I was blessed with an understanding of some of the deeper implications of God's self-identifying "I AM," spoken to Moses from a burning bush when he asked God, "What is your name?" (Exod. 3:13–14). Appellation of the All in all, iconic in its utterance and utterly devoid of image, this name signifies the untouchable and unimaginable, or so I had been taught. It is awe-inspiring, existential, not at all warm and welcoming, not a name indicative of intimacy, of One who would draw us close.

Then one day, inspired by the Spirit, I imagined that I AM was meant to be an invitation, not an exclamation. I AM... — two words followed by an ellipsis, as if to say, this is incomplete. You fill in what follows. I do not think God intended I AM to be definitive, a conversation stopper. I think God spoke an unfinished phrase, a formula for naming that necessitates our response. I AM...who?...what? Who do you say that I am? Who would you wish that I am? Through a sensitive, loving, relational invitation, God waits to hear what aspect of divinity we want to call upon, what dimension of goodness or justice will fulfill our present need. In essence God is saying: I am...patience; I am...strength; I am...courage; I am...peace; I am...comfort...compassion...healing...hope. God is saying to each of us, whatever you need me to be for you, I will be that for you. I will be what you name. Yes, I will be for you who you want me to be. I will be for you who you need me to be. Call upon me from the depth of your need and I will be there for you. Call to me by any name you choose, and I will hear the name and the need and I will answer you. Evocative, unconditionally conditional, I AM is God's self-disclosure that is forever in process, promising us there will always be another metaphor, another revelation, another song to sing.

I sometimes wonder how I got to where I am, considering where I started from. The theological fascination is inexplicable, the love of words self-evident, but what about the music? Although never a profession, it has always lingered on the cusp of my senses beckoning to be explored. I was seven when I started piano lessons. Sister Claveria at my parish school announced in catechism class one day that she was looking for students. The cost of a lesson was fifty cents. It wasn't hard to convince my parents to let me learn from her. My dad played violin and loved classical music. I was told I could use the old upright in the corner of the cavernous dance hall at the back of my grandfather's saloon. After my first lesson, my relatives crowded around the piano and asked me to play something for them. Their standard was the gypsy fiddler who played at the bar from time to time. Play a Hungarian czardas, they said. I showed them middle C, and the third and fifth above it. They were not impressed. I practiced diligently every day, and eventually moved from saloon to salon with a new teacher, an expensive one, and a piano of my own.

Miss Wallace charged three dollars for a thirty-minute lesson, which was a big sacrifice for my parents in those days. Students had to come to her house. I was sure it was because she was a recluse and never left her home. She always wore dark glasses and rarely said a word. To enter her house was to step into a room full of fringe, dark-toned tapestries, a musty smell, and dim light, a parlor where the shades were always drawn, then into a big conservatory where the largest piano I had ever seen sat and waited for me. In time I was able to accompany my dad as he played the violin. We enjoyed those times together. However, my heart was elsewhere. Larry, who was a kid at school, didn't have to read the notes. He played without music, played chords by ear that had everyone singing familiar tunes and songs that were popular. That was how I wanted to play. I had enough sense not to risk raising the subject with Miss Wallace and pleaded with my dad to find someone to teach me to play like that. To his credit he made an effort once, but it was half-hearted and unsuccessful, and we never spoke of it again. Just before entering high school, I quit taking piano lessons, and one day, I stopped playing. All my extracurricular time went into other things.

Singing was something else. When I was in elementary school, we put on a musical called "Taffy Ann." I was given the title role, and I didn't even know I could sing. I suppose it was because I would have no trouble memorizing the music. My biggest concern was not my voice but the color of my hair. It had to be the color of taffy — that was the whole point of the play — and my hair was barn-door brown. My mom went out and bought some tint to wash highlights into it and, I might add, right out of it again, a procedure that had us laughing until tears came to our eyes. I can't believe I actually sang on a stage in front of all those people. I was reticent in those days. I don't know what it sounded like, but I felt like a Broadway star. I recall vividly another student older than myself who sang like an angel. Her voice was so clear, so beautiful. I could tell that she was trained. How I wished I too could sing like that. When I asked her where she had studied, she said her teacher was Miss Wallace. I couldn't believe my ears. I begged my mom and dad to let me take singing lessons too, which would mean another three dollars. Reluctantly, they agreed. My dad went with me to discuss the possibility with my teacher. She whisked me to the piano, sat down, played a chord, and asked me to sing a phrase. I did, and then she said, "Stick to the piano," and that was the end of that.

Years later, in another world, after I had my music degree and was at a loss to know what I was going to do with it, I began singing folk-style songs for my own spirit's nurture and to enhance our liturgies. A choir of sisters joined me. Sister Clement had a gift for spontaneous harmony and we filled in chords around her. It was exhilarating and fun. Someone said we should make a record, but I had no intention of becoming a singing nun. Then one day several key members of the choir received assignments overseas, to Vietnam and to Bangladesh, which was then East Pakistan. Now or never, I was told, and thanks to Sister Pierre, who was adamant that a recording should be made, we found ourselves in a studio taping *Joy Is Like the Rain*. We cut two albums that same day in approximately seven hours, while sitting on the floor, because that was how we had always rehearsed back at the motherhouse. The producers could not believe their ears or, for that matter, their eyes. They kept calling their friends to come have a look. A steady stream of people appeared behind the little window of the sound engineering room. It must have been a sight to see, eleven "nuns" in habits and veils sitting on the floor of the RKO Studios in downtown Manhattan singing Scripture songs. I shudder at our audacity. We had only fifteen songs prepared and we needed twenty-four. It was an exhausting day, but when the final note was sounded, we had two albums. *I Know the Secret* followed *Joy Is Like the Rain.*

Much to my amazement, the songs took off on a path of their own and invited me to follow them into the homes and sanctuaries of countless Christian communities in this country and abroad. In 1967 I found myself on the stage of Carnegie Hall for the first ecumenical concert in the hall's venerable history, honing what had been a hobby into a genuine call. I never did get used to the response the music generated, and every letter I have received has always been a lovely surprise. I remember one in particular that came in 1966 from a pilot in a medical unit in Vietnam.

"While standing the night helicopter medical evacuation watch here at the Marble Mountain Air Facility in Vietnam, I heard a Voice of America program on your activities, which contained selections from your album *Joy Is Like the Rain.* I have never heard music in a modern idiom so clearly express and project a religious spirit. For the joy and renewal of calm faith which this music brought to me, I thank you." Two years later he wrote again, this time from his home in Hawaii. "Since the night I heard *Joy Is Like the Rain* . . . I have never heard the record again. No matter: I never *needed* to hear it as much as I did that night. The weather was so bad that only emergency med-evacs were being assigned as missions, and those only at 'pilot's discretion.' Following the Voice of America program we got three such missions, two of which were into 'hot' zones. I honestly believe that had it not been for the effect *Joy Is Like the Rain* had on me, I would have aborted these missions prior to completion. As it developed, we successfully completed all three missions, and I have often wondered what the reaction of the marines and Vietnamese civilians who were evacuated that night would be if they knew that their delivery to the hospital, and consequent recovery, was due primarily to the music of a group of sisters in Philadelphia, Pa." Enclosed was an order for the album, so that he could share the songs with his family. One more letter arrived that year, just before Christmas. It read: "Some time ago I sort of made a bargain with the Lord that I would share with the Medical Mission Sisters 50 percent of the profits realized during this year from my investment." Enclosed was a check for $425.80. The letter was also signed by his wife and their three young children.

That letter, along with many others, pushed me in the direction of a full-time ministry of the word in song. Loretta, Jane, Mary Elizabeth, and I formed a group in 1971 that toured the United States and Canada for eighteen months in a ministry of music, liturgy, and prayer. While presenting a workshop at Mc-Master Divinity School in Ontario, I received an invitation to come for graduate studies, and I decided it was time for a serious introduction to Protestant theologians and biblical scholarship. In exchange for their generous financial support, I helped form a student choir with guitars and contemporary music and turned several Baptist services into full-blown liturgies. Even the president's daughter was doing liturgical dance. From there I went to Princeton Theological Seminary to study for a Ph.D. My dissertation — published under the title *Why Sing?* — focused on a consideration of the theology underlying sacred music in the Roman Catholic tradition. What I found was mostly aesthetics posing as theology and a lengthy tradition of regulations based on

papal precedent with no solid theological rationale. It was heart-
ening to discover that the people's song, which I dearly loved,
had ancient and respectable roots, in fact had solid biblical roots,
and was a vitally important element of sacramental liturgy recovered by Vatican II. I finished the degree and, once again, went
on to other things, too much to tell in this small book. In the
intervening years, I began to think differently about so many
things. Those paradigm shifts are reflected in the evolution of
my song.

I am finally learning to play by ear on an old upright piano. It
is summer, the windows are open wide, and as my fingers sound
the chords, a third generation of chipmunks scamper just a few
feet away and a hundred songbirds sing. They can't resist the
music. I laugh as I sing along. I sing songs *of* God and I sing songs
to God in praise of all things living, and day after day life itself is
a song that sings to me. It is an uninterrupted song, for its energy
pulsates through me even when I am not singing, which truth
be told is most of the time, though I wish it were otherwise. It
is in the day's unfolding that I know the spirit of the living God
is reaching out to me, suggesting themes for my soul's expan-
sion, inspiring variations, showing me where I might improvise or
proceed unaccompanied.

One day, not so very long ago, when I was in the shower,
with the waters of life flowing over me and wisdom waters within
me, I heard as clear as a bell the words, "it is all one." I knew
in an instant the source of the voice and the message it meant
to convey. The consciousness of the cosmos, the spirit of all life
come and gone, confirmed what I already knew deep down on
the cellular level and had begun to share with others. All is
one. We are all one. The cosmos, our planet, all people are one.
God and we are one. One living, loving spirit. In that Spirit we
are one.

Yesterday, when I went for my walk at five o'clock in the
morning, I saw a mound on the seminary lawn across the street

from my doorway. There's a homeless person, I surmised, under
that pile of blankets and tarp, with that wire basket filled with
stuff and those bundles there beside it. After I had circled back,
I decided that breakfast would be a nice way for the person to
start the day. I prepared a peanut-butter-and-jelly sandwich on
a big deli roll of a size a hungry man would welcome, added
a banana, a chocolate covered cookie, and a tall cold glass of
milk. I had planned to tiptoe over, place the paper plate on the
grass, and quietly slip away, but as I approached the person sat
up and turned to look at me. Much to my amazement, I saw a
woman, not a man. She seemed too young to be on the street,
although it was hard to tell her age. She was gentle, gracious, and
thanked me. I smiled, blessed her, and let her be, convinced that
if she wanted something more, she would be back and so would I,
and I would know where to find her. I couldn't help but wonder,
why is she out here on the ground? What is her story? What is
her need? What message for me is hidden within this seemingly
chance encounter? I had been startled when I saw her face. She
looked a lot like me.

All that I think and feel about things of lasting significance
make their way into song. Milestone moments that stretch every
facet of my being reside in keepsake metaphors that I revisit from
time to time in gratitude and praise. We grow together, the song
and I, in comprehending the meaning of our shared destiny. I
never know when I will be pulled into some unseen dimension
to wrestle with the Spirit inhabiting all that lives and moves and
has essential being. When thoughts get too convoluted, when
prose cannot seem to handle what the heart cries out to express,
I listen for the music. As metaphor meets melody and rhymes
and rhythms intersect, the pulse of a world beyond our world
resonates within me. I let go, let Spirit lead, and savor the experience. The sung word and the poetic word arise from an oasis
somewhere inside where I go to integrate life and love, pain and
disappointment, and a passion for possibilities. This sanctuary,

this sacred place is like a parallel universe, where Spirit resides, where love beckons, and I fly away.

The Bible speaks of a New Song, a metaphor for the living God and for the One who is to come, the Christ here among us. The new song of the new creation is sounding all around us and in that place within us — GodSong in a simple mode in a key anyone can play. I am not really a musician. I am not really a composer. I am just a singer of simple songs who knows that the call to be who I am is a call that comes from God.

In New Testament times, there was this understanding re-garding the word of God. The word proclaimed, the word's proclaimer, and the act of proclaiming were one. May it be so in our own times when we sing the word of God.

I pray that in the songs we sing, alone or all together, we will hear the Spirit singing. For then our song is God's song in us, our singing is God's spirit singing through us. When the singer and the song and the singing are one, rejoice and give thanks to God.

> *You spoke a word and stirred a silent spring.*
> *You touched my heart and I began to sing,*
> *to free the music deep in everything.*
> *Now all the earth with its innate melody*
> *has meaning for me forever.*
> > *You are the song and You are the singing.*
> > *All through the longing, You come bringing music.*
>
> *You promised You would give the words to say.*
> *You touched my heart and I began to pray,*
> *and all my frail defenses fell away,*
> *and all the walls that held my feelings inside*
> *were thrown open wide forever.*
> > *You are the prayer and You are the praying.*
> > *When I prepare, You're there conveying music.*

You promised to be present everywhere.
You touched my heart and I became aware
of all the love entrusted to my care,
and of the need to share the gift that You give,
the love that will live forever.
  You are the gift and You are the giving.
  We are uplifted, You are living . . .

  You are the song and You are the singing.
  All through the longing, You come bringing music.
  You are the gift and You are the giving.
  We are uplifted, You are living music.

O — Holy One, I sing Your praise.
O — Ancient One, how wise Your ways.

All around and deep within the world Your all-pervading Spirit
manifests Your power and Your presence, Your life, Your love.

O — Everlasting One, for You I long.
O — Co-creating One, my strength, my song.

Everywhere Your web of life gives witness to imagination,
echoing Your whispered word proclaiming that all are one.

O — Revealing One, that I may see.
O — Healing Presence healing me.

Everywhere Your wholesome Spirit pulsates with divine intention,
taking all our timeless moments into eternity.

O — One who comes, I know You're near.
O — One who is already here.

All around and deep within my soul I sense Your centering Spirit,
energy transforming me, till one day my heart is whole.

O — Immortal One, come dwell in me.
O — Incarnate One, how blessed are we.
O — Eternal Presence, blessed be!

— Summer 1998

Come, you will see, I will be
all you require, all you desire forever.
I am the Spirit of
life everlasting, of
all of the love you give, all in you that lives on.
　　You are the melody, I am the word of our song.
　　Sing to Me, sing of Me, and I will be singing along.

Look everywhere. You will see Me.
I am life lived all around and in you.
I am the surging seas.
I am the galaxies,
linking infinity to humanity now.
　　You are the melody, I am the word of our song.
　　Sing to Me, sing of Me, and I will be singing along.

Draw near to Me. I will reveal
what is real in all the press upon you.
Yes, I'll be there for you.
Yes, I will care for you,
so that you too may know My compassionate love.
　　You are the melody, I am the word of our song.
　　Sing to Me, sing of Me, and I will be singing along.

Come, you will see Spirit of life
and of love, look for Me deep within you.
I am integrity.
I am serenity.
I will give meaning to every song that you sing.
　　You are the melody, I am the word of our song.
　　Sing to Me, sing of Me, and I will be singing along.

—Summer 1998

I want to express my gratitude to all who have helped me grow in spirit along the paths Spirit has led me and for all the nurturing contexts that have encouraged creativity and ritual celebration. To my family and my community, my colleagues, associates, students, and friends, thank you for believing in both the singer and the song.

Acknowledgments

Some of the narratives and reflections in this book originally appeared in a monthly column in *The American Catholic – Northeast*, an independent regional newspaper published in Farmington, Connecticut. "Take the Time" first appeared in *Fellowship in Prayer* (February 1988).

Songs cited in the text have been recorded and published as sheet music in the following collections. Those titles marked with an asterisk (*) are also included in *Songlines*, an anthology of hymns, songs, rounds, and refrains.

"Peter" (p. 6) — *I Know the Secret*

"The Wedding Banquet" * (p. 7) — *Joy Is Like the Rain*

"You Are the Song" * (pp. 9, 174) — *WomanSong*

"Joy Is Like the Rain" * (pp. 6, 9) — *Joy Is Like the Rain*

"Don't Worry" (p. 14) — *I Know the Secret*

"Long Road to Freedom" * (p. 25) — *Joy Is Like the Rain*

"Night" * (p. 30) — *Knock, Knock*

"How I Have Longed" * (p. 34) — *Joy Is Like the Rain*

"Architect of All Creation" * (p. 40) — *SpiritSong*

"Angels" * (p. 43) — *SpiritSong*

"The Visit" * (p. 48) — *WomanSong* and *Knock, Knock*

"Take the Time" * (p. 53) — *WomanSong*

"Starlight" (p. 58) — *EarthSong*

"Once Upon a Morning Star" * (p. 58) — *EarthSong*

"Living Water" * (p. 65) — *WomanSong* and *Sandstone*

"We Are the Word" * (p. 75) — *WomanSong*

"What Do You Ask of Me?" * (p. 87) — *Remember Me*

"Spirit of God, Feed Me, Fill Me" * (p. 95) — *EarthSong*

"Come, Sophia" * (p. 106) — *Hymns Re-Imagined*

"We Praise You, God" * (p. 127) — *EarthSong*

"Loving You" * (p. 136) — *Sandstone*

"Mother and God" * (p. 148) — *WomanSong*

"Wisdom" (p. 151) — *SpiritSong*

"Mystery" * (pp. 158, 163) — *WomanSong*

"God of My Childhood" * (p. 165) — *EarthSong*

"I Sing Your Praise"(p. 176) — *SpiritSong*

"SpiritSong" (p. 177) — *SpiritSong*

The two recordings by the Voices of Joy Gospel Choir, *Voices of Joy* and *More Voices of Joy,* are available from the Medical Mission Sisters at 77 Sherman Street, Hartford, CT 06105.